Don,

To remind you
of some interesting
tastes and
conversations.

Good fortune,

Douglas

June 2000

The Original
Malt Whisky
Almanac

A Taster's Guide
Wallace Milroy

Neil Wilson Publishing • Glasgow • Scotland

Published by Neil Wilson Publishing Ltd
303a The Pentagon Centre
36 Washington Street
GLASGOW
G3 8AZ
Tel: 0141-221-1117
Fax: 0141-221-5363
E-mail: nwp@cqm.co.uk
http://www.nwp.co.uk/

First edition published July 1986.
Second edition published June 1987.
Reprinted August 1987, January, October 1988.
Third edition published September 1989.
Reprinted June, September 1990.
Fourth edition published April 1991.
Reprinted August, November 1991, March 1992.
Fifth edition published November 1992.
Reprinted March, December 1993, April 1994, March 1995.
Sixth edition published November 1995.
Reprinted July 1996.
Reprinted March 1999.

A catalogue record for this book is available from the British Library.
ISBN 1-897784-68-6
Printed by Bookprint, Barcelona, Spain

Contents

Acknowledgements

It is now over 10 years since the first edition of this pocket guide was produced and it is heartening to note that many of the people who helped me then are still involved in the industry. To all of you, my grateful thanks as ever. Particular thanks to the staff at Glengoyne Distillery who put up with me when we took the cover photograph! You have no idea how cold it was in that bond! Also, my thanks to Derek Kingwell who acted as food consultant on the book.

NWP gratefully acknowledges the assistance of the Keepers of the Quaich in the production of this work.

USEFUL ADDRESSES

The Scotch Whisky Association
14 Cork Street
LONDON W1X 1PF
Tel: 0171-629-4384

Scotch Whisky Heritage Centre
354 Castlehill
Royal Mile
EDINBURGH EH1 2NE
Tel: 0131-220-0441
Fax: 0131-220-6288

Adult admission £4.95, concessionary rates available. Audio-visual, guided tours, gift shop, tasting bar, self-service restaurant, infrared headsets in 8 languages.

The Scotch Malt Whisky Society
The Vaults
87 Giles Street
Leith, EDINBURGH EH6 6BZ
Tel: 0131-554-3451

Cash-strength bottlings with regular newsletter, Member's Room and flats, countrywide tastings, whisky school. £50 membership fee includes a free bottle of malt.

Foreword

Wallace Milroy's *Original Malt Whisky Almanac*, now in its 7th edition, is the *vade mecum* for all those many folk at home and abroad who would like to know about our Scotch malt whiskies – be it from the simpler facts to the more detailed aspects of production of the distilleries and where they are located.

This handy but encyclopaedic tome is, by its very nature, as much part of the Highlander's dress as is his sporran.

I, as the present Grand Master of the Keepers of the Quaich, can only repeat the words of my predecessors who have extolled its virtues by highly commending it to all who embark on the ever pleasant adventure of enjoying Scotland's finest and most unique product.

The Duke of Argyll, J.P.
Grand Master
Keepers of the Quaich
Inveraray Castle
January, 1998

Introduction

IN the introduction to the last edition of this book you may recall that my main topic of discussion was the continuing inequality on duty charged on spirits in the EU and further afield. This situation has since altered dramatically, and in the case of Japan, it will have far-reaching consequences for Scotch whisky. On the 1st October 1997 Scotch whisky received a 44% reduction in taxation in Japan amounting to 300 Yen (£1.60) per bottle. In anticipation of this, exports were 9% higher in the first half of 1997 at nearly 20 million bottles. Following on the heels of this there has been a further reduction of 26% in May 1998. All this has to be good news for Scotch whisky exports to Japan...but there is a cloud on the horizon – the abolition of duty-free retailing within the EU.

While the EU has maintained the position that discriminatory duties on spirits are not a priority, it has decided that duty-free outlets are to be abolished from the 30th June 1999. The effect of this on the Scotch industry and the cost of air travel and tourism, will be serious. In order to make up the loss, Edinburgh Airport alone would need to increase landing charges by 15%, but it would still have an annual shortfall of £22 million. The result would mean a curtailment of planned expansion with a detrimental effect on the airport's ability to attract new routes...something which the new Scottish Parliament will view as an embarrassment at the very least. Surely the EU cannot have it both ways? To ban duty-free sales is short-sighted given the disparity of taxation on spirits which continues to exist throughout the 15 member states. And what of the effect on the Scotch whisky industry?

When duty free goes it is estimated that some 700 jobs in the industry in Scotland will go with it, many of them in high unemployment areas such as the Highlands and the West of Scotland. If there is one retail area in which competition is not distorted in the EU it is in duty free and until the effects of the banning of duty free sales have been fully looked into, this vital component of trade (worth around £2.9 billion throughout the EU) should be allowed to remain. In the meantime the Scotch Whisky Association will continue to needle and lobby Brussels in defence of duty free.

On a more welcome note, the sales of Scotch abroad continue to rise. Spain has now leapfrogged France as the second most important overseas market and

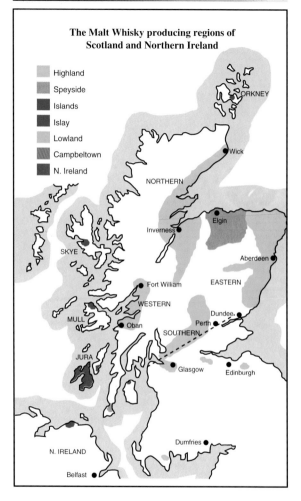

The Malt Whisky producing regions of Scotland and Northern Ireland

- Highland
- Speyside
- Islands
- Islay
- Lowland
- Campbeltown
- N. Ireland

ORKNEY

Wick

NORTHERN

Elgin

Inverness

SKYE

Aberdeen

Fort William

EASTERN

WESTERN

Dundee

MULL

Oban

Perth

SOUTHERN

JURA

Glasgow

Edinburgh

Dumfries

N. IRELAND

Belfast

annual sales to the USA, our largest market abroad, have passed the £300 million mark for the first time. Some concern has to be expressed regarding the strength of Sterling abroad, but the overall 5% increase in value of sales is a great achievement.

Thought For Food

When we launched the second edition of this book at Claridges in London, we enjoyed a five-course lunch with a malt from United Distillers' Malt Cellar (the forerunner to the Classic Malts) accompanying each course and I have since believed that distillers should encourage the consumption of fine malts with fine food. Whereas the complexities of a wine can often be defeated by the strong flavours and textures of some foods, single malt whisky's sheer concentration of flavours can complete and complement many foodstuffs. In Scotland, trying local specialities wherever possible with regional malts is an ideal combination. After all, they have both been developed and produced in the same climatic conditions. The addition of water – rather than simply diluting the nose and palate – enhances and awakes the malt's hidden delights. This offers a more realistic accompaniment and can be served in a similar quantity to that of wine in a glass. The late Sir Fitzroy Maclean of Dunconnel used to drink nothing but Scotch and water at large dinners, particularly when he was unsure of the wine, and he never complained in the morning!

In the regional introductions I have suggested some combinations of malts and foods that are well suited to each other. Treat my suggestions as a guide, however, and do try any cheese, particularly our own Scottish varieties, with any malt wherever possible. You may be amazed at the results.

Whisky on the Web

The Internet is a source of a great deal of information on Scotch whisky and I have made a selection of URL's which offer a range of interactive whisky experiences. These can be found at the rear of the book on page 155 and I accept no liability whatsoever for their contents, suffice to say that the last time I looked at them, they were very informative! There is little doubt that the Internet is helping to spread the word about Scotch by allowing far-flung enthusiasts the opportunity to discuss malt through this intriguing medium.

Finally, my thanks to the Keepers of the Quaich who have once more supported production of this new edition.

Wallace Milroy
London, May 1998

KEY TO SYMBOLS

✉   Address

℡   Telephone number

🖷   Fax number

🏛   Reception Centre and tour arrangements

🎥   Audio-visual

♿   Disabled access

♿◢   Restricted disabled access

🎁   Gift shop

🍶   Tastings

⚗   Number of wash stills

⚗   Number of spirit stills

🛢   Cask woods used for maturation

🏛   Type of maltings

ABBREVIATIONS

IWSC   International Wine and Spirit Competition

ROSPA   Royal Society for the Prevention of Accidents

ASVA   Association of Scottish Visitor Attractions

STB   Scottish Tourist Board

Visiting distilleries

Never have Scotland's distilleries been so well equipped to deal with the curious tourist or the informed traveller. When my publisher arranged for the cover photograph to be taken at Glengoyne Distillery, I was struck by the professional and informative manner in which a group of Spanish customers was taken through the distillery. Everything was explained to them in their own language, from the audio-visual introduction, through the tour of the distillery to the well-stocked shop. This experience would have been unheard of in 1980, but now it is commonplace throughout the country.

These distilleries have received a great deal of investment in order to cope with the seasonal influx of visitors and are now considered a must on the list of attractions to visit. Furthermore anyone with an interest in whisky, who feels that their knowledge on the subject is complete, would do well to drop in on any of the venues listed below and indulge in a short refresher course. There is nothing like the real thing to blow the cobwebs away!

Even the remoter plants will offer a welcome dram, and perhaps a small exhibition or video in a side-room. In every case, the sincerity of the welcome is heartfelt, so don't be put off by what might appear to be a lack of facilities. The staff of Scotland's distilleries are always keen to promote their own drams. For example, the remote Islay distillery, Caol Ila, so magnificently situated on the Sound of Islay, continues to deal with over 2,000 visitors a year; Scotland's smallest distillery at Edradour is coping admirably with 100,000 while the largest at Tomatin in the north is being vistited by 70,000 per annum. Still at the top of the league is Glenturret near Crieff, which catered for 228,416 in 1996.

Another major point of interest for the enthusiast is Speyside Cooperage (tel: 01340-871108, fax: 01340-881303) which is on the Speyside Malt Whisky Trail and can be found on the Dufftown Road, Craigellachie, AB38 9RS. It is open all year, Monday to Friday, from 09.30 to 16.30 and from June to September it also opens on Saturdays between the same hours. Audio-visual facilities have just been installed and a tasting area is under construction as we go to press. Admission is £2.25 for adults and £1.75 for children and concessions.

As in the previous edition, I have set out on a regional basis those companies and distilleries which offer facilities, further details of which can be found under the actual distillery entries. Distilleries which are on the Malt Whisky Trail are marked with an asterisk.

ALLIED DISTILLERS LTD

A company much transformed in recent years, and now tied up with the Spanish Domecq group, Allied have yet to invest as heavily in visitor reception centres as some of their competitors.

Region	Distillery	Page No
Speyside	Glendronach	39
Eastern Highlands	Glencadam	83
Islay	Laphroaig	115

BEN NEVIS DISTILLERY (Fort William) LTD

Japanese ownership has seen an investment made in this west-coast reception centre which still continues to draw some 30,000 visitors per annum.

Region	Distillery	Page No
Western Highlands	Ben Nevis	95

BURN STEWART DISTILLERS PLC

Tobermory is now dealing with some 8,000 visitors passing through Mull. The distillery is situated at the entrance to the port.

Region	Distillery	Page No
Islands	Tobermory	129

CAMPBELL DISTILLERS LTD

This French-owned company is now concentrating on Edradour's unique character as Scotland's smallest distillery, situated on the hillside outside Pitlochry.

Region	Distillery	Page No
Southern Highlands	Edradour	89

CO-ORDINATED DEVELOPMENT SERVICES LTD

Raymond Armstrong's Northern Ireland based company has breathed new life into Bladnoch and it is now a thriving facility near Wigtown, Scotland's designated Booktown. The distillery will be producing again in 1998.

Region	Distillery	Page No
Lowlands	Bladnoch	100

GLENMORANGIE PLC

The Glenmorangie Distillery, situated in a beautiful part of Easter Ross, should not be missed out. The recent purchase of Ardbeg has also resulted in the establishment of reception facilities there. A nice wee jaunt down the road after you've been in to visit Laphroaig!

Region	Distillery	Page No
Northern Highlands	Glenmorangie	76
Islay	Ardbeg	108

HIGHLAND DISTILLERS

The mergers and acquisitions of the last few years have extended the number of distilleries in this company's portfolio, but only two reception centres are currently operating, albeit with one of them at Glenturret, the busiest of all in Scotland.

Region	Distillery	Page No
Southern Highlands	Glenturret	91
Islands	Highland Park	125

HISTORIC SCOTLAND

Not a producer as such, but Historic Scotland have a 30-year tenure of one of Scotland's distilleries and are therefore very much involved in promoting the heritage of the industry. The distillery in their care is perfectly preserved and is now a protected monument. The last cask of Dallas Dhu, distilled in 1983, is now on sale here.

Region	Distillery	Page No
Speyside	Dallas Dhu*	30

IRISH DISTILLERS LTD

Now wholly French-owned but very definitely remaining Irish in spirit, the company continues to offer visitors to Old Bushmills on the beautiful Co Antrim coast a very rewarding time at the UK's oldest licensed distillery.

Region	Distillery	Page No
Northern Ireland	Old Bushmills	131

ISLE OF ARRAN DISTILLERS LTD

The new visitors' centre drew around 40,000 visitors in its first season and a target of 100,000 is achievable judging by the facilities on offer at Lochranza.

Region	Distillery	Page No
Islands	Lochranza	124

JIM BEAM BRANDS (GREATER EUROPE) PLC

This Glasgow-based, American-owned company has always concentrated on their one reception facility in the east and have no plans to extend their investment to any of their other distilleries at present.

Region	Distillery	Page No
Eastern Highlands	Fettercairn	84

J&G GRANT

One of the essential stops when visiting Speyside, if only for the fact that this is still a family-owned business and likely to remain so.

Region	Distillery	Page No
Speyside	Glenfarclas*	42

LANG BROS LTD

Closely associated with Highland Distillers and The Erdrington Group Ltd, this long-established company manages what is perhaps the best distillery to visit while in the Glasgow area, if only for its location beneath the Campsie Fells. The facilities are now open all year round.

Region	Distillery	Page No
Southern Highlands	Glengoyne	90

THE MACALLAN DISTILLERS LTD

With only one distillery in the company's portfolio, this firm has invested wisely in their HQ building at Easter Elchies, Craigellachie and if you are one of the lucky ones able to sample this wonderful whisky in its own setting, you will not be disappointed.

Region	Distillery	Page No
Speyside	Macallan	55

MORRISON BOWMORE DISTILLERS LTD

Upgraded retail facilities and a priceless situation offer a very complete experience for the visitor. Although Islay remains relatively remote in terms of road and ferry access, remember that it is only a 30-minute flight from Glasgow.

Region	Distillery	Page No
Islay	Bowmore	109

SEAGRAM DISTILLERS

With their five-year Heritage Programme almost complete, Seagram have focused their efforts around their Speyside distilling operations and have undertaken restoration and development work on projects directly related to the whisky-making traditions of the area. The result of this has been dramatic with the development of the Heritage Centre at Strathisla, the restoration of Linn House in Keith and the Glen Grant Gardens at the distillery in Rothes.

Region	Distillery	Page No
Speyside	Glen Keith	34
	Glen Grant*	33
	Glenlivet*	45
	Strathisla*	62

TOMATIN DISTILLERY CO LTD

Gradual development of the facilities has brought a significant increase in the number of visitors who want to have a look at one of the largest distilleries in Scotland.

Region	Distillery	Page No
Northern Highlands	Tomatin	80

UNITED DISTILLERS & VINTNERS (UDV)

Following the merger of Grand Met and Guinness, this company has consolidated its position as Scotland's largest producer of malt whisky. With this comes the largest portfolio of visitor centres in the trade.

Region	Distillery	Page No
Speyside	Cardhu*	26
	Cragganmore	27
Northern Highlands	Clynelish	71
	Dalwhinnie	73
	Glen Ord	75
Eastern Highlands	Royal Lochnagar	85
Southern Highlands	Blair Athol	87
Western Highlands	Oban	96
Lowlands	Glenkinchie	101
Islay	Lagavulin	114
Islands	Talisker	128

WILLIAM GRANT & SONS LTD

Although now operating three distilleries within Dufftown, one well-developed reception centre services all the company's requirements. It is largely based around the Glenfiddich experience, with Kininvie and Balvenie remaining a little in the background. Dufftown is one of the best places to visit to appreciate the scale of distilling in Scotland when the late-Victorian boom occurred.

Region	Distillery	Page No
Speyside	Glenfiddich*	43

WILLIAM LAWSON DISTILLERS LTD

As we go to press the the sell-off of the Dewar's brand and the related distilling activity at Craigellachie, Aultmore, Royal Brackla and Aberfeldy is subject to EU and FTC approval. On the basis that the distilleries do change hands, I am listing the one distillery which did accept visitors when it was in UDV's ownership.

Region	Distillery	Page No
Southern Highlands	Aberfeldy	86

Speyside

OR many whisky enthusiasts malt whisky is most closely associated with Speyside, but in truth this is only half the story. The strength of the association, however, can be seen from the many distilleries which, although not situated beside the River Spey, make allegiance with it when stating their provenance.

The River Livet has also suffered from the same back-handed compliment and over the years many distillers claimed to produce 'a Glenlivet', when strictly speaking they were stretching not only the geographical boundaries a bit far, but also the patience of the owners of The Glenlivet Distillery itself. It all goes to show how over the last two centuries 'Speyside' has stood for the highest possible quality, and today the truth of that statement has not diminished at all.

The trade, however, has always tended to look at the large number of distilleries situated in this area as simply 'Speysides', and I have continued with this categorisation in this edition. As you will see from the accompanying map on page 16, the 'Golden Triangle' really does exist, stretching from Elgin over towards Banff and down to the cradle of distilling on Speyside – Dufftown. In this area lies the greatest concentration of malt whisky-making apparatus in the world, and to savour the atmosphere here is to realise how important and how dearly distilling is valued in the Highlands of Scotland.

The success of the Speyside distillers is due to the production of high-quality illicit whisky. At the end of the 18th century, their whisky was in such demand that the 'protected' Lowland markets were gradually infiltrated by their smuggled produce. Finally, in 1823, an Act of Parliament betrayed the fact that the Government had at last realised the best way to reduce the illicit trade was to make it attractive for the distillers to go legal. The Speyside men were, however, suspicious and only after George Smith, who distilled in Glenlivet, went legal in 1824 did they begin to accept the new laws.

Smith's foresight is manifested in the industry on Speyside as it stands today where over 50 malt distilleries are in operation.

The recent merger of Grand Metropolitan and Guinness to form Diageo, has meant that more distilleries are coming under one corporate umbrella, which,

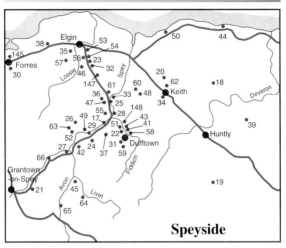

DISTILLERY LOCATION NUMBERS REFER TO PAGE NUMBERS

some might say, could be bad for business because it allows for further reviewing of capacity. However, this has also directly led to the selling off of four distilleries, two of which are located in Speyside. Craigellachie and Aultmore are in the process of being taken over by Bacardi and this will undoubtedly secure the long-term presence of these units. Other distilleries have also moved to new ownership, such as Balmenach, which has been taken over by Inver House Distillers. These developments can only be good for the maintenance of a healthy and varied malt distillery portfolio in Scotland.

I am still not listing Allt a'Bhainne, Braes of Glenlivet or Strathmill due to their lack of general availability but I do intend to carry them in the next edition. Kininvie at Dufftown has been producing for a few years now and I have recently sampled a five-year-old which is detailed on page 51.

Thought for Food

Speyside single malts are best suited to poultry, game birds, rich fruit cakes and puddings. Here are three ideas, all of them equally delicious.

Glen Grant 10-year-old and roast guinea fowl stuffed

with apple, pear and leek.

Knockando and wild boar casserole.

Macallan 10-year-old and Christmas pudding.

BRAND	**Aberlour**
✉	ABERLOUR, Banffshire AB38 9PJ
☎	01340-871204/285
🖷	01340-871729
MANAGER	Alan J. Winchester
OWNING COMPANY	Campbell Distillers Ltd
PRODUCTION STATUS	Operational
ESTABLISHED	1826, rebuilt 1879
SOURCE	St Drostan's Well
🛢	Ex-bourbon and sherry
🍾	2
🍾	2

🏭

📖

Visitors by appointment.

AGE WHEN BOTTLED	10 years
STRENGTH ABV	40, 43 & 57.1%
SPECIAL BOTTLINGS	15-y.o sherry finish; 100 proof @ 57.1%; 21-y.o sherry matured; Aberlour a'Bunadh (unfiltered cask strength)
EXPORT BOTTLINGS	Antique @ 43%; 15-y.o Mary Queen of Scots; 21-y.o sherrywood-matured Special Reserve

TASTING NOTES	10 years, 43%
NOSE	Full and rich with hints of sherry and a heather-honey sweetness. A delicate aroma of smoke.
TASTE	Elegant, medium-bodied, soft, appealing balance which finishes cleanly and smoothly with a refreshing after-taste.
COMMENTS	A most eminent malt. Three-times Gold Medal winner in the IWSC

BRAND	**An Cnoc**
DISTILLERY	Knockdhu
✉	KNOCK, Aberdeenshire AB5 5LJ
☎	01466-771223
📠	01466-771359
MANAGER	Stanley Harrower
OWNING COMPANY	Knockdhu Distillery Co., Ltd.
PRODUCTION STATUS	Operational
ESTABLISHED	1893-4
SOURCE	Five springs on the Knock Hill
🛢	Hogsheads
🔥	1
🔥	1

AGE WHEN BOTTLED	12 years
STRENGTH ABV	40%

TASTING NOTES

NOSE A distinctive soft aroma of fruit with a hint of smoke.

TASTE Very refined with a mellow smooth, fruity, peach-like softness and a long finish.

COMMENTS An excellent all-round malt. This distillery was the first bought by The Distillers Co to supply malt whisky for their own use. This malt was previously marketed as Knockdhu.

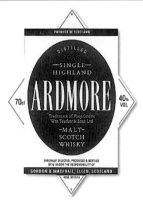

MALT	**Ardmore**
	✉ KENNETHMONT, Aberdeenshire AB54 4NH
	☏ 01464-831213
	🖷 01464-831428
MANAGER	Calcott Innes Harper
OWNING COMPANY	Allied Distillers Ltd
PRODUCTION STATUS	Operational
ESTABLISHED	1899
SOURCE	Springs on Knockandy Hill
	🛢 Ex-bourbon
	🍶 4
	🍶 4

TASTING NOTES	1981, 40%
NOSE	A light aroma.
TASTE	Big, sweet and malty on the palate with a good, crisp finish.
COMMENTS	After-dinner dram. A limited edition bottling is sometimes available from Wm Teacher at 15 years and 45.7%. See pages 153-154.

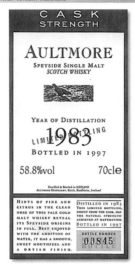

CASK STRENGTH

AULTMORE

SPEYSIDE SINGLE MALT
SCOTCH WHISKY

YEAR OF DISTILLATION
1983
LIMITED BOTTLING
BOTTLED IN 1997

58.8%vol   70cle

Distilled & Bottled in SCOTLAND
AULTMORE Distillery, Keith, Banffshire, Scotland

HINTS OF PINE AND
CITRUS IN THE CLEAN
NOSE OF THIS PALE GOLD
MALT WHISKY REVEAL
ITS SPEYSIDE ORIGINS
IN FULL. BEST ENJOYED
WITH THE ADDITION OF
WATER, IT HAS A SMOOTH,
SWEET MOUTHFEEL AND
A DRYISH FINISH.

DISTILLED IN 1983
THIS LIMITED BOTTLING,
DIRECT FROM THE CASK, HAS
THE NATURAL STRENGTH
ACHIEVED AT MATURATION.
BOTTLED IN 1997

BOTTLE NUMBER
00845

BRAND	**Aultmore**
✉	KEITH, Banffshire AB55 6QY
☎	01542-882762
🖷	01542-886467
MANAGER	Jim Riddell
OWNING COMPANY	William Lawson Distillers Ltd
PRODUCTION STATUS	Operational
ESTABLISHED	1897
SOURCE	Auchinderran Burn
🛢	Ex-bourbon
🌡	2
🌡	2

AGE WHEN BOTTLED	12 years
STRENGTH ABV	43%
SPECIAL BOTTLINGS	1983 @ 58.8%

TASTING NOTES	
NOSE	A delightful, fresh aroma with a sweet hint and a touch of peat.
TASTE	Smooth, well-balanced with a fruity palate and a mellow, warming finish.
COMMENTS	Now generally available as a brand and suitable as an after-dinner malt.

SPEYSIDE
SINGLE MALT
SCOTCH WHISKY

Sometime in the early 19th, after walking
in the CROMDALE hills with
his 2 BROTHERS, James McGregor settled
and established

BALMENACH

distillery. Spring water runs beneath those
same HILLS is still used to produce
this RICH flavoured single MALT SCOTCH
WHISKY of exemplary quality.

AGED **12** YEARS

43% Vol   70 cl

BRAND	**Balmenach**
⊠	Cromdale, GRANTOWN-ON-SPEY, Morayshire PH26 3PF
☎	01479-872569
MANAGER	Graeme Hutcheon
OWNING COMPANY	Inver House Distillers Ltd
PRODUCTION STATUS	Operational
ESTABLISHED	c1824
SOURCE	Cromdale Burn
🛢	Ex-bourbon
🔥	3
⚗	3

AGE WHEN BOTTLED	12 years
STRENGTH ABV	43%

TASTING NOTES

NOSE	Light, attractive, sweet, nutty aroma with floral overtones and a slight hint of smoke.
TASTE	Starts quite full and firm, then lingers softly with a sweet, nutty, vanilla finish.
COMMENTS	An extremely well-balanced and satisfying drink.

BRAND	**The Balvenie**
✉	Dufftown, KEITH, Banffshire AB55 4DH
☎	01340-820373
📠	01340-820805
MANAGER	Bill White
OWNING COMPANY	Wm Grant & Sons Ltd
PRODUCTION STATUS	Operational
ESTABLISHED	1892
SOURCE	The Robbie Dubh springs
🛢	Ex-bourbon and sherry
⌂	Floor maltings
🍺	4
🍺	4

AGE WHEN BOTTLED	10, 12, 15 & 21 years
STRENGTH ABV	10, 12 & 21-y.o: 40%; 15-y.o: 50%
SPECIAL BOTTLINGS	Double Wood: 12 years; Single Barrel: 15 years; Port Wood Finish: 21 years

TASTING NOTES	12-year-old, Double Wood
NOSE	Excellent well-pronounced aroma.
TASTE	Big, distinctive flavour. Almost a liqueur and a very distinct honey-sweet aftertaste.
COMMENTS	A connoisseur's malt for after-dinner. The Double Wood is matured in two types of wood: traditional oak and then sherried oak. The Single Barrel is a single distillation bottled from a single cask, forming a limited edition of no more than 300 hand-numbered bottles.

BENRIACH DISTILLERY
EST.1898
A SINGLE
PURE HIGHLAND MALT
Scotch Whisky

Benriach Distillery, in the heart of the Highlands,
still malts its own barley. The resulting whisky has
a unique and attractive delicacy
PRODUCED AND BOTTLED BY THE

BENRIACH
DISTILLERY C⁰
ELGIN, MORAYSHIRE, SCOTLAND, IV30 3SJ
Distilled and Bottled in Scotland

AGED 10 YEARS

70cl ℮ 43%vol

BRAND	**Benriach**
✉	Longmorn, ELGIN, Morayshire IV30 3SJ
☎	01542-783400
🖷	01542-783404
MANAGER	Bob MacPherson
OWNING COMPANY	Seagram Distillers
PRODUCTION STATUS	Operational
ESTABLISHED	1898. Closed 1900. Re-established 1965.
SOURCE	Local springs
🛢	Ex-bourbon
⛁	Floor maltings
🍶	2
🍶	2

AGE WHEN BOTTLED	10 years
STRENGTH ABV	43%

TASTING NOTES	
NOSE	Light, sweet and delicate with a hint of fruit.
TASTE	Medium-bodied yet complex with a combined delicacy of flowering currants and peat. Delicate, dry, refined aftertaste.
COMMENTS	A Heritage Selection malt from Chivas.

SPEYSIDE
SINGLE MALT
SCOTCH WHISKY

BENRINNES

distillery stands on the
northern shoulder of BEN RINNES
700 feet above sea level.
It is ideally located to exploit
the natural advantages of the
area-pure air, peat and
barley and the finest of hill water,
which rises through granite
from springs on the summit
of the mountain. The resulting
single MALT SCOTCH WHISKY,
is rounded and mellow.

AGED 15 YEARS

Distilled & Bottled in SCOTLAND.
BENRINNES DISTILLERY
Aberlour, Banffshire, Scotland

43% vol 70cl

BRAND		**Benrinnes**
	✉	ABERLOUR, Banffshire AB38 9NN
	☎	01340-871215
	📠	01340-871840
MANAGER		Alan Barclay
OWNING COMPANY		UDV
PRODUCTION STATUS		Operational
ESTABLISHED		c1835
SOURCE		Rowantree and Scurran Burns
	🛢	Ex-bourbon
	♨	2
	♨	2
AWARDS RECEIVED		ROSPA Health & Safety Gold Award 1997

AGE WHEN BOTTLED	15 years
STRENGTH ABV	43%
SPECIAL BOTTLINGS	1980 @ 61%; 1974 @ 60.4% Rare Malts Selection

TASTING NOTES	
NOSE	A delightful, sweet and flowery aroma.
TASTE	Firm, positive with a hint of blackberry fruitiness. It has a liqueur-like quality with a clean, fresh taste which lingers.
COMMENTS	An excellent after-dinner dram.

CONNOISSEURS CHOICE

Connoisseurs Choice, a range of single malts from various distilleries of Scotland.

The distilleries situated in the area of the valley of the River Spey produce some of the finest malt whiskies.

GRAMPIANS

SINGLE SPEYSIDE
MALT SCOTCH WHISKY
DISTILLED AT

CAPERDONICH
DISTILLERY
Proprietors: The Glenlivet & Glen Grant Distilleries Ltd

DISTILLED **1980** DISTILLED

SPECIALLY SELECTED, PRODUCED AND BOTTLED BY
70cl   GORDON & MACPHAIL   40%vol
ELGIN · SCOTLAND
PRODUCT OF SCOTLAND

MALT	**Caperdonich**
✉	ROTHES, Morayshire AB38 7BS
☎	01542-783300
MANAGER	Willie Mearns
OWNING COMPANY	Seagram Distillers
PRODUCTION STATUS	Operational
ESTABLISHED	1898. Closed 1902. Re-established 1965.
SOURCE	The Caperdonich Burn
🛢	Ex-bourbon and sherry
⚗	2
⚗	2

AGE WHEN BOTTLED	1980
STRENGTH ABV	40%

TASTING NOTES	
NOSE	A light, very delicate fragrance of peat.
TASTE	Medium, slight hint of fruit with a fragrant, quick smoky finish.
COMMENTS	The distillery is across the road from Glen Grant and used to be called Glen Grant No 2. See pages 153-154.

BRAND	**Cardhu**
	(Kaar-doo)
✉	ABERLOUR, Banffshire AB38 7RY
☏	01340-810204
🖷	01340-810491
MANAGER	Charlie Smith
OWNING COMPANY	UDV
PRODUCTION STATUS	Operational
ESTABLISHED	1824
SOURCE	Springs on the Mannoch Hill and the Lyne Burn
🛢	Ex-bourbon and sherry
♨	3
♨	3

📷 ☏	01340-810204
🖷	01340-810491
	Mar to Nov, Mon-Fri: 09.30-16.30. Easter to Sept, Sat: 09.30-16.30. July to Sept, Sun: 11.00-16.00. Dec to Feb, by appointment. Groups by appointment only. Admission charge redeemable in shop.
VISITORS PER YEAR	16,000

AGE WHEN BOTTLED	12 years
STRENGTH ABV	40%

TASTING NOTES	
NOSE	A hint of sweetness and fruit with an excellent, fragrant, smoky bouquet.
TASTE	Smooth, mellow flavour of apples and nuts with a delightful long-lasting finish. Sweet overtones.
COMMENTS	A good after-dinner dram which is now one of UDV's most popular.

BRAND	**Cragganmore**
✉	BALLINDALLOCH, Banffshire AB37 9AB
☎	01807-500202
🖷	01807-500288
MANAGER	Mike Gunn
OWNING COMPANY	UDV
PRODUCTION STATUS	Operational
ESTABLISHED	1869
SOURCE	The Craggan Burn
🛢	Ex-bourbon
🍶	2
🍶	2

(⚒)

☎	01807-500202
🖷	01807-500288
	Trade visitors and public by appointment only.
VISITORS PER YEAR	2,000

AGE WHEN BOTTLED	12 years
STRENGTH ABV	40%
SPECIAL BOTTLINGS	1978 @ 60.1%; Distiller's Edition, 1984

TASTING NOTES	.
NOSE	Light, delicate honey nose with dry overtones.
TASTE	A refined, well-balanced distillate. Quite firm with a malty, smoky taste which finishes quickly.
COMMENTS	One of UDV's Classic Malt range.

SPEYSIDE
SINGLE MALT
SCOTCH WHISKY

CRAIGELLACHIE

distillery, founded in 1888, in the county of BANFFSHIRE, stands overlooking the RIVER SPEY, the rock of Craigellachie, and TELFORD'S single span iron BRIDGE. The distillery uses local spring water running from little CONVAL HILL for mashing, resulting in this excellent single MALT SCOTCH WHISKY of light and smoky character.

AGED 14 YEARS

43% vol   70 cl

BRAND	**Craigellachie**
✉	Craigellachie, ABERLOUR, Banffshire AB38 9ST
☎	01340-881212/881228
🖷	01340-881311
MANAGER	Charlie Smith
OWNING COMPANY	William Lawson Distillers Ltd
PRODUCTION STATUS	Operational
ESTABLISHED	1891
SOURCE	Little Conval hill
🛢	Ex-bourbon
♨	2
♨	2

🏭

Open all year, Mon-Fri, by appointment only.

AGE WHEN BOTTLED	14 years
STRENGTH ABV	43%
SPECIAL BOTTLINGS	16-y.o @ 59.3%; 22-y.o @ 60.2%; Rare Malts Selection

TASTING NOTES	
NOSE	Pungent, smoky aroma of peat.
TASTE	Light-bodied, smoky flavour. More delicate on the palate than the nose suggests. Good character with length.
COMMENTS	An interesting after-dinner dram.

CASK STRENGTH

DAILUAINE

SPEYSIDE SINGLE MALT
SCOTCH WHISKY

YEAR OF DISTILLATION
LIMITED 1980 ING
BOTTLED IN 1997

63.0%vol   70cle

Distilled & Bottled in SCOTLAND
Dailuaine Distillery, Carron, Aberlour, Banffshire, Scotland

THIS MAHOGANY DARK
SPEYSIDE MALT HAS A
STRONG NOSE WITH TRACES
OF TOFFEE, OLOROSO
SHERRY AND DARK RUM.
BEST ENJOYED WITH THE
ADDITION OF WATER, ITS
RICH MEDIUM-SWEET
FLAVOURS LEAD TO A
LONG, DRY FINISH.

DISTILLED IN 1980
THIS LIMITED BOTTLING,
DIRECT FROM THE CASK, HAS
THE NATURAL STRENGTH
ACHIEVED AT MATURATION.
BOTTLED IN 1997

BOTTLE NUMBER
00236

BRAND	**Dailuaine**
	(Dale-yoo-in)
✉	Carron, ABERLOUR, Banffshire AB38 7RE
☎	01340-810361
🖷	01340-872504
MANAGER	Alan Barclay
OWNING COMPANY	UDV
PRODUCTION STATUS	Operational
ESTABLISHED	1851
SOURCE	Bailliemullich Burn
🛢	Ex-bourbon
🛢	3
🛢	3

AGE WHEN BOTTLED	16 years
STRENGTH ABV	43%
SPECIAL BOTTLINGS	22-y.o @ 60.9%; 17-y.o @ 63%

TASTING NOTES	22-year-old, 60.9%
NOSE	Full, rich, fruity aroma with honeysuckle overtones.
TASTE	Full of flavour which draws out a rich, dry sweetness to perfection.
COMMENTS	An excellent after-dinner dram from UDV's Rare Malts Selection.

MALT	**Dallas Dhu**
	(Dallas doo)
✉	Mannachie Road, FORRES, Morayshire IV36 0RR
OWNING COMPANY	UDV, in the care of Historic Scotland.
PRODUCTION STATUS	Closed 1983. Can be reinstated.
ESTABLISHED	1899. No longer licensed.
SOURCE	Altyre Burn
🛢	Ex-bourbon and sherry
⚗	1
⚗	1

🏭

♨✈◼♿	
☎	01309-676548
	Apr to Sept, 09.30-18.30, last admission at 18.00. Sun: 14.00-18.30. Oct to Mar, 09.30-16.30, last admission at 16.00. Sun: 14.00-18.30. Closed Thu PM and Fri.
VISITORS PER YEAR	18,000

AGE WHEN BOTTLED	21 years
STRENGTH ABV	61.9%
SPECIAL BOTTLINGS	Final cask from 1983 is being bottled at around £195.

TASTING NOTES	24-year-old, 59.9%
NOSE	Really rich and full, interwoven with oak smoke, sweetness and malt.
TASTE	Rich, full, clinging and malty with every element in harmony. Finished most beautifully with haunting traces of oak.
COMMENTS	Now a successful and popular 'living' museum under the stewardship of Historic Scotland. This dram is exceptional and is currently bottled at a number of ages and strengths as a UDV Rare Malts Selection. A splash of water is essential.

RARE MALTS
SELECTION

Each individual vintage has been specially selected from Scotland's
finest single malt stocks of rare or now silent distilleries.
The limited bottlings of these scarce and unique whiskies are at
natural cask strength for the enjoyment of the true connoisseur.

NATURAL
CASK STRENGTH
SINGLE MALT
SCOTCH WHISKY

AGED **21** YEARS

DISTILLED 1975
DUFFTOWN-GLENLIVET
DISTILLERY
ESTABLISHED 1896
DUFFTOWN,BANFFSHIRE
54.8%vol 70cl℮
PRODUCED AND BOTTLED
IN SCOTLAND
LIMITED EDITION
BOTTLE
SEPTEMBER 1997   Nº   5250

BRAND	**Dufftown**
✉	Dufftown, KEITH, Banffshire AB55 4BR
☎	01340-820224
🖷	01340-820060
MANAGER	Steve McGingle
OWNING COMPANY	UDV
PRODUCTION STATUS	Operational
ESTABLISHED	1896
SOURCE	Jock's Well in the Conval Hills
🛢	Ex-bourbon
🛢	3
🛢	3

AGE WHEN BOTTLED	15 years
STRENGTH ABV	43%
SPECIAL BOTTLINGS	1975 @ 54.8% Rare Malts Selection

TASTING NOTES
NOSE   Light, flowery, pleasant aroma with a hint of fruit.
TASTE   A round, smooth sweet taste of fruit taste which tends
                     to linger on the palate. A splendid, full aftertaste.
COMMENTS   Pre-dinner.

BRAND	**Glen Elgin**
✉	Longmorn, ELGIN, Morayshire IV30 3SL
☎	01343-860212
🖷	01343-862077
MANAGER	Ian Millar
OWNING COMPANY	UDV
PRODUCTION STATUS	Operational
ESTABLISHED	1900
SOURCE	Local springs near Milbuies loch
🛢	Ex-bourbon
🜹	4
🜹	3

AGE WHEN BOTTLED	1968
STRENGTH ABV	40%
SPECIAL BOTTLINGS	1976 @ 46.3%

TASTING NOTES	
NOSE	Agreeable aroma of peat, heather and honey.
TASTE	Medium-weight touch of heather honey and hint of smokiness with an excellent, firm finish.
COMMENTS	The best of both worlds, an excellent all-round malt, suitable for drinking at any time.

BRAND	**Glen Grant**
	✉ ROTHES, Morayshire AB38 7BS
	☎ 01542-783300
	🖷 01542-783306
MANAGER	Willie Mearns
OWNING COMPANY	Seagram Distillers
PRODUCTION STATUS	Operational
ESTABLISHED	1840
SOURCE	The Caperdonich Well
	🛢 Ex-bourbon and sherry
	🗝 4
	🗝 4

🏚	🏚♥▢
	☎ 01542-783318
	🖷 01542-783304
	Mid-March to end May, Mon-Sat: 10.00-16.00. Sun: 11.30-16.00. June to Sept, Mon-Sat: 10.00-17.00. Sun: 11.30-17.00. Oct, Mon-Sat: 10.00-16.00. Sun: 11.30-16.00. Groups by appointment. Redeemable admission charge.
OTHER ATTRACTIONS	The Victorian Glen Grant Garden
VISITORS PER YEAR	21,000

AGE WHEN BOTTLED	10 years
STRENGTH ABV	40%
EXPORT BOTTLINGS	43%

TASTING NOTES	
NOSE	Light, dry aroma. Slightly astringent.
TASTE	Dry flavour, light trace of fruit on the palate.
COMMENTS	A fine malt – preferably pre-dinner. Hugely popular in Europe.

BRAND	**Glen Keith**
	✉ Station Road, KEITH, Banffshire AB55 3BU
	☎ 01542-783044
	📠 01542-783056
MANAGER	Norman Green
OWNING COMPANY	Seagram Distillers
PRODUCTION STATUS	Operational
ESTABLISHED	1957-60
SOURCE	Balloch Hill springs
🛢	Ex-bourbon and sherry
🔥	3
🔥	3

	☎ 01542-783044
	📠 01542-783056
	By appointment only.

AGE WHEN BOTTLED	1983
STRENGTH ABV	43%

TASTING NOTES	
NOSE	Good, medium aroma with a light aromatic sweetness with a hint of oak.
TASTE	Gentle, dry aromatic fruitiness with a subtle, full length of warmth and fruit.
COMMENTS	A Heritage Selection malt from Chivas.

BRAND	**Glen Moray**
✉	ELGIN, Morayshire IV30 1YE
☎	01343-542577
🖷	01343-546195
MANAGER	Edwin Dodson
OWNING COMPANY	Glenmorangie plc
PRODUCTION STATUS	Operational
ESTABLISHED	1897
SOURCE	River Lossie
🛢	Ex-bourbon
🔥	2
🔥	2

(H)

Visitors are welcome. Phone in advance.

AGE WHEN BOTTLED	12, 16 years
STRENGTH ABV	40%
SPECIAL BOTTLINGS	Centenary bottling of 12-year-old.

TASTING NOTES	12-year-old, 40%
NOSE	Fresh, light aroma
TASTE	Light, pleasant, smoky and malty with a clean finish. A fine all-round malt.
COMMENTS	A pre-dinner dram available in regimental tins representing the Black Watch and the Queen's Own Cameron Highlanders.

MALT	**Glen Spey**
	✉ ROTHES, Morayshire AB38 7AY
	☏ 01340-831215
	🖷 01340-831356
MANAGER	Peter Warren
OWNING COMPANY	UDV
PRODUCTION STATUS	Operational
ESTABLISHED	c1878
SOURCE	The Doonie Burn
	🛢 Ex-bourbon
	⚗ 2
	⚗ 2

TASTING NOTES	15-year-old, 62.2%
NOSE	Strikingly aromatic and fragrant.
TASTE	Very full palate, strong overtones of ripe fruit and a light, smokiness which finished smoothly.
COMMENTS	An after-dinner dram which needs a good splash of water. See pages 153-154.

Vintage 1985
Single Highland Malt Scotch Whisky
Matured in oak casks for 11 years
Distilled at Glenallachie Distillery
on 11.10.85   Bottled 11.96°
Cask Nos. 4072 - 74   Bottle No.   of 872
This whisky has been selected, produced and bottled in
Scotland for and under the sole responsibility of
Signatory Vintage Scotch Whisky Co. Ltd.
70cl   Edinburgh EH6 8PY Scotland   43% vol

MALT	**Glenallachie**
	✉ ABERLOUR, Banffshire AB38 9LR
	☎ 01340-871315/710
	🖶 01340-871711
MANAGER	Robert Hay
OWNING COMPANY	Campbell Distillers Ltd
PRODUCTION STATUS	Operational
ESTABLISHED	1967-8
SOURCE	Springs on Ben Rinnes
	🛢 Ex-bourbon
	🍾 2
	🍶 2

TASTING NOTES	12-year-old, 43%
NOSE	Very elegant with a delightful, floral bouquet.
TASTE	Smooth-bodied with a hint of honey and fruit and a light, sweet finish. Extremely well-balanced.
COMMENTS	The distillery was built by W. Delmé-Evans (see also Jura and Tullibardine) for Charles Mackinlay & Co Ltd. A vastly underrated malt only available from the independent bottlers, if at all. See pages 153-154.

Vintage 1975
Single Highland Malt Scotch Whisky
Matured in oak casks for 22 years
Distilled at Glenburgie Distillery
on 3.6.75   Bottled 17.9.97
Cask No. 6007   Bottle No.   of 265
This whisky has been selected, produced and bottled in
Scotland for and under the sole responsibility of
Signatory Vintage Scotch Whisky Co. Ltd.
70cl   Edinburgh EH6 &PY Scotland   56.6%vol

MALT	**Glenburgie**
✉	FORRES, Morayshire IV36 OQU
☎	01343-850258
🖷	01343-850480
MANAGER	Brian Thomas
OWNING COMPANY	Allied Distillers Ltd
PRODUCTION STATUS	Operational
ESTABLISHED	1810
SOURCE	Local springs
🛢	Mainly ex-bourbon barrels
🍾	2
🥃	2

🏠

	By appointment only.
OTHER ATTRACTIONS	A very attractively landscaped location.
VISITORS PER YEAR	100

TASTING NOTES	8-year-old, 40%
NOSE	A fragrant, floral aroma with hints of fruit.
TASTE	A light, delicate, aromatic flavour of honey and maple leaf with a pleasant finish.
COMMENTS	An extremely good pre-dinner malt, but only from the independent bottlers. See pages 153-154.

BRAND	**The Glendronach**
✉	Forgue, HUNTLY, Aberdeenshire AB54 6DB
☎	01466-730202
🖷	01466-730202
MANAGER	Calcott Innes Harper
OWNING COMPANY	Allied Distillers Ltd
PRODUCTION STATUS	Operational
ESTABLISHED	1826
SOURCE	Private springs
🛢	European oak, seasoned or ex-sherry
⌂	Floor maltings
🝆	2
🝆	2

🏭

♨ ♥ ▣ 🕭

☎ 01466-730202

🖷 01466-730313

Shop open during office hours. Tours at 10.00 or 14.00 all year. Group bookings by appointment.

OTHER ATTRACTIONS	The floor maltings and the traditional coal-fired stills.
AWARDS RECEIVED	1997 IWSC Silver Medal
VISITORS PER YEAR	4,000

AGE WHEN BOTTLED	15 years
STRENGTH ABV	40%
SPECIAL BOTTLINGS	1987 @ 43%
EXPORT BOTTLINGS	43% (except Canada)

TASTING NOTES	15-year-old, 40%

NOSE	Smooth aroma with a light trace of sweetness.
TASTE	Well-balanced, lingering on the palate with smoky overtones and a long, light, sweet aftertaste.
COMMENTS	A good dram, after-dinner and much sought after.

SPEYSIDE
SINGLE MALT
SCOTCH WHISKY

GLENDULLAN

distillery, located in a beautiful *wooded*
valley was ℔ built in 1897 and is one of seven
established in *Dufftown* in the C19th.
The River Fiddich flows past the *distillery*;
originally *providing power* to drive
machinery, it is now used ℔ for cooling.
GLENDULLAN is a firm, mellow *single MALT
SCOTCH WHISKY* with a fruity
bouquet and a smooth *lingering* finish.

AGED **12** YEARS

Distilled & Bottled in *SCOTLAND*
GLENDULLAN DISTILLERY
Dufftown, Keith, Banffshire, Scotland.

43% vol   **70 cl**

BRAND	**Glendullan**
✉	Dufftown, KEITH, Banffshire AB55 4DJ
☎	01340-822300
🖶	01340-822302
MANAGER	Steve McGingle
OWNING COMPANY	UDV
PRODUCTION STATUS	Operational
ESTABLISHED	1897-8
SOURCE	River Fiddich
🛢	Ex-bourbon and sherry
🍶	3
🍶	3

AGE WHEN BOTTLED	12 years
STRENGTH ABV	43%
SPECIAL BOTTLINGS	8-y.o @ 40%; 23-y.o @ 58.6% Rare Malts Selection

TASTING NOTES	
NOSE	Attractive, fruity bouquet. Full of promise.
TASTE	Firm, mellow with a delightful, nutty finish and a smooth, honeyed lingering aftertaste.
COMMENTS	A good after-dinner malt.

BRAND	**Glenfarclas**
	✉ Marypark, BALLINDALLOCH, Banffshire AB37 9BD
	☎ 01807-500209
	🖷 01807-500234
MANAGER	Mr J. Miller
OWNING COMPANY	J&G Grant
PRODUCTION STATUS	Operational
ESTABLISHED	1836
SOURCE	Springs on Ben Rinnes
	🛢 Ex-sherry and bourbon
	🍶 3
	🍶 3

🏭	🚻 ♥ ■ ♿
	☎ 01807-500257
	🖷 01807-500234
	Apr to Sept, Mon-Fri: 09.30-17.00. Oct to Mar, Mon-Fri: 10.00-16.00. June to Sept, Sat: 10.00-16.00, Sun: 12.30-16.30. Last tour one hour before closing time. Charge: £2.50, partly redeemable in shop.
OTHER ATTRACTIONS	The 'Ship's Room' from the *Empress of Australia*.
AWARDS RECEIVED	1996 International Spirits Challenge: Outright Winner – 30-y.o.

AGE WHEN BOTTLED	10, 15, 21, 25 & 30 years
STRENGTH ABV	40% for 10-y.o; 60% for '105'
EXPORT BOTTLINGS	8-y.o @ 40%; 12-y.o @ 43%; 1970/76/78 @ cask strength.

TASTING NOTES	15-year-old, 46%
NOSE	A rich, tantalising, delicious promise.
TASTE	Full of character and flavour. Sweet overtones of ripe, luscious fruit.
COMMENTS	Wonderful, fulfilling drinking from a great Speyside distillery.

BRAND	**Glenfiddich**
✉	Dufftown, KEITH, Banffshire AB55 4DH
☎	01340-820373
📠	01340-820805
MANAGER	Bill White
OWNING COMPANY	Wm Grant & Sons Ltd
PRODUCTION STATUS	Operational
ESTABLISHED	1886-7
SOURCE	The Robbie Dubh Springs
🛢	Ex-bourbon and sherry
🔥	10
🔥	18

🏭	🚹 🍴 🖼 ♿
☎	01340-820373
📠	01340-820805
	Easter to mid-Oct, Mon-Sat: 09.30-16.30. Sun: 12.00-16.30. Mid to Oct to Easter, Mon-Fri: 09.30-16.30. Closed Xmas/New Year. Groups of more than 12, please phone in advance. PR manager: Elizabeth Lafferty.
OTHER ATTRACTIONS	Picnic area. AV is in six languages.
VISITORS PER YEAR	120,000

AGE WHEN BOTTLED	8 years minimum
STRENGTH ABV	40%
SPECIAL BOTTLINGS	50-y.o @ 43%; Cask Strength, 15-y.o @ 51%
EXPORT BOTTLINGS	43%

TASTING NOTES	
NOSE	A light, delicate, fresh touch of peat.
TASTE	Attractive flavour with a sweet follow-through. Well-balanced and stimulating.
COMMENTS	A fine introduction to malt whisky.

MALT	**Glenglassaugh**
✉	PORTSOY, Banffshire AB45 2SQ
☏	01261-842367
OWNING COMPANY	Highland Distillers
PRODUCTION STATUS	Mothballed
ESTABLISHED	1875
SOURCE	The Glassaugh Spring
🛢	Ex-bourbon
🗝	1
🗝	1

TASTING NOTES	1983, 40%
NOSE	Light, fresh and delicate. Slightly sweet.
TASTE	Charming. A hint of sweetness which is full of promise with a delicious, dry, smooth follow-through.
COMMENTS	For drinking at any time, but only available from the independent bottlers. See pages 153-154.

BRAND	**The Glenlivet**
	✉ BALLINDALLOCH, Banffshire AB37 9DB
	☎ 01542-783220
	🖷 01542-783220
MANAGER	Jim Cryle
OWNING COMPANY	Seagram Distillers
PRODUCTION STATUS	Operational
ESTABLISHED	1824
SOURCE	Josie's Well
	🛢 Ex-bourbon and sherry
	♂ 4
	♂ 4

🏛	🎟 ♥ ▣ ♿
	☎ 01542-783220
	🖷 01542-783220
	Mid-March to end Oct, Mon-Sat: 10.00-16.00. Sun: 12.30-16.00. July & Aug, Mon-Sun: 10.00-18.00. Groups by appointment. Redeemable admission charge.
AWARDS RECEIVED	18-y.o: 1995 IWSC: Best malt over 12 years old. 1996 IWSC, Gold Medal.
VISITORS PER YEAR	75,000

AGE WHEN BOTTLED	12 & 18 years
STRENGTH ABV	12-y.o: 40%; 18-y.o: 43%
SPECIAL BOTTLINGS	The Archive.
EXPORT BOTTLINGS	43%

TASTING NOTES	12 years, 40%
NOSE	A light, delicate nose with plenty of fruit.
TASTE	Medium to light trace of sherry sweetness. Quite full on the palate.
COMMENTS	A first-class malt. One of the most popular malts in the world – deservedly so.

SPEYSIDE
SINGLE MALT *SCOTCH* WHISKY

The three *spirit* stills at the

GLENLOSSIE

distillery have purifiers installed between the lyne arm and the condenser. This has a bearing on the character of the single MALT SCOTCH WHISKY produced which has a fresh, grassy aroma and a smooth, lingering flavour. Built in 1876 by John Duff, the distillery lies four miles south of ELGIN in Morayshire.

AGED **10** YEARS

43% vol   70 cl

BRAND	**Glenlossie**
✉	Birnie, ELGIN, Morayshire IV30 3SS
☎	01343-860331
🖷	01343-860302
MANAGER	Harry Fox
OWNING COMPANY	UDV
PRODUCTION STATUS	Operational
ESTABLISHED	1876
SOURCE	The Bardon Burn
🛢	Ex-bourbon
⚗	3
⚗	3

AGE WHEN BOTTLED	10 years
STRENGTH ABV	43%

TASTING NOTES

NOSE	A soft touch of sweetness with sandalwood overtones.
TASTE	A long-lasting smoothness with a delicate almond-like finish.
COMMENTS	An after-dinner dram from a remote location near Elgin.

THE GLENROTHES DISTILLERY
SAMPLE ROOM

700ml

43% vol.

CHARACTER: *Ripe, fruity, vanilla notes*

CHECKED: *J.C. Stevens* DATE: 1/4/82

APPROVED: *R.H. Feind* DATE: 20.8.96

DISTILLED IN

1982

BOTTLED IN 1996

SCOTCH WHISKY

Distilled and Bottled in Scotland. Berry Bros. & Rudd, 3 St James's St, London
PRODUCT OF SCOTLAND

BRAND	**The Glenrothes**
✉	ROTHES, Morayshire AB38 7AA
☎	01340-831248
📠	01340-831484
OWNING COMPANY	Highland Distillers
PRODUCTION STATUS	Operational
ESTABLISHED	1878
SOURCE	Local springs
🛢	Ex-bourbon and sherry
🛢	5
🛢	5
AWARDS RECEIVED	1997 IWSC Silver Medal, Best Malt Over 21 years (1972 bottling)

AGE WHEN BOTTLED	1972, 1982
STRENGTH ABV	43%

TASTING NOTES	1982, 43%
NOSE	A rich, subtle fragrance of sherry with a light hint of smoke.
TASTE	Excellent balance of soft fruit and malt with an exquisite length of flavour and a smooth, long-lasting finish.
COMMENTS	A limited release of vintage Glenrothes from Berry Bros & Rudd.

MALT	**Glentauchers**
	✉ Mulben, KEITH, Banffshire AB55 23L
	✆ 01542-860272
	📠 01542-860327
MANAGER	Ronnie MacDonald
OWNING COMPANY	Allied Distillers Ltd
PRODUCTION STATUS	Operational
ESTABLISHED	1898
SOURCE	Rosarie Burn
	🛢 Ex-bourbon
	🥃 3
	🥃 3
VISITORS PER YEAR	25

TASTING NOTES	1979, 40%
NOSE	Light, sweet aroma of honey and spice.
TASTE	Lightly flavoured with a mellow, soft, dry finish.
COMMENTS	A pre-dinner dram from another distillery founded at the end of the 19th-century. See pages 153-154.

40% vol.   *Product of Scotland*   70 cl.

IMPERIAL

TRADEMARK OF PROPRIETORS: ALLIED DISTILLERS LTD

Single Highland Malt

Scotch DISTILLED 1979 Whisky

IMPERIAL
Built in *1897*, the year of Queen Victoria's Diamond Jubilee, the Imperial Distillery stands majestically among the dark woods of Carron, in a fold of the hills which encompass the glittering Spey.

Specially selected, produced and bottled by and under the responsibility of *Gordon & Macphail*, Elgin, Scotland. Regd. Bottler.

MALT	**Imperial**
✉	Carron, ABERLOUR, Morayshire AB38 7QP
☎	01340-810276
📠	01340-810563
MANAGER	Ronnie MacDonald
OWNING COMPANY	Allied Distillers Ltd
PRODUCTION STATUS	Operational
ESTABLISHED	1897
SOURCE	Aldach Springs
🛢	Ex-bourbon
🌡	2
🌡	2

TASTING NOTES	1979, 40%
NOSE	Delightful – rich and smoky.
TASTE	Rich and mellow with an absolutely full and delicious finish.
COMMENTS	One of the great underrated malts. Try it after-dinner. See pages 153-154.

SPEYSIDE
SINGLE MALT
SCOTCH WHISKY

The *Oyster-Catcher* is a common sight
around the

INCHGOWER

distillery, which stands *close* to the *sea*
on the mouth of the *RIVER SPEY*
near *BUCKIE. Inchgower,*
established in 1824, produces one of the
most *distinctive single malt* whiskies
in *SPEYSIDE.* It is a malt for the
discerning drinker ~ a *complex* aroma
precedes a *fruity, spicy*
taste *☺* with a hint of *salt.*

AGED **14** YEARS

43% vol   70cl

BRAND	**Inchgower**
✉	BUCKIE, Banffshire AB56 5AB
☎	01542-831161
🖷	01542-834531
MANAGER	James Riddell
OWNING COMPANY	UDV
PRODUCTION STATUS	Operational
ESTABLISHED	1871
SOURCE	Springs in the Menduff Hills
🛢	Ex-bourbon
♂	2
♀	2

AGE WHEN BOTTLED	14 years
STRENGTH ABV	43%
SPECIAL BOTTLINGS	22-y.o @ 55.7% Rare Malts Selection

TASTING NOTES

NOSE	Very distinctive with a pleasant hint of peat and a malty sweetness.
TASTE	Good, distinctive flavour finishing with a pronounced light sweetness.
COMMENTS	A well-balanced malt. After-dinner.

MALT	**Kininvie**
✉	Dufftown, KEITH, Banffshire AB55 4DH
☏	01340-820373
📠	01340-820805
MANAGER	Bill White
OWNING COMPANY	Wm Grant & Sons Ltd
PRODUCTION STATUS	Operational
ESTABLISHED	1990
SOURCE	The Robbie Dubh springs
🛢	Ex-bourbon
⌕	2
⌕	6

TASTING NOTES	5 years, cask strength
NOSE	Distinctive aroma of smoke and walnuts. Mellow and sweet.
TASTE	Even at this young age a dry, smooth, richness is noticeable with hints of oak and smoke. Finishes promisingly.
COMMENTS	If this fine malt becomes available in years to come it will be well received.

BRAND	**Knockando**
✉	Knockando, ABERLOUR, Morayshire AB38 7RD
☏	01340-810205
📠	01340-810369
MANAGER	Innes Shaw
OWNING COMPANY	UDV
PRODUCTION STATUS	Operational
ESTABLISHED	1898
SOURCE	Cardnach spring
🛢	Ex-bourbon
🍾	2
🍾	2

🏭

☏   01340-810205
Trade visitors only.

AGE WHEN BOTTLED	13 years
STRENGTH ABV	43%

TASTING NOTES

NOSE   Full, pleasant aroma of hot butter and spicy nuts.

TASTE   Medium-bodied with a pleasant syrupy flavour which, despite finishing quite quickly, is satisfying.

COMMENTS   After-dinner. Bottled when it is considered ready, rather than at a pre-determined age. The label carries dates of distillation and bottling, currently 1984 and 1997 respectively.

BRAND	**Linkwood**
	✉ ELGIN, Morayshire IV30 3RD
	☎ 01343-547004
	🖷 01343-549449
MANAGER	Ian Millar
OWNING COMPANY	UDV
PRODUCTION STATUS	Operational
ESTABLISHED	1825
SOURCE	Springs near Milbuies Loch
🝫	3
🝫	3

AGE WHEN BOTTLED	12 years
STRENGTH ABV	43%
SPECIAL BOTTLINGS	23-y.o @ 61.2% Rare Malts Selection; 1983 @ 59.8%

TASTING NOTES	
NOSE	Slightly smoky with a trace of sweetness which gives it a refined appeal.
TASTE	Full-bodied hint of fruit with a smoky, harmonious finish.
COMMENTS	One of the best malts available. Don't pass this one by.

BRAND	**Longmorn**
	✉ ELGIN, Morayshire IV30 3SJ
	☎ 01542-783400
	📠 01542-783404
MANAGER	Bob McPherson
OWNING COMPANY	Seagram Distillers
PRODUCTION STATUS	Operational
ESTABLISHED	1894-5
SOURCE	Local springs
	🍶 4
	🍶 4

(⋔)

	☎ 01542-783042
	By appointment only.
AWARDS RECEIVED	1994 IWSC: Gold Medal. 1995/96 IWSC: Silver Medal.

AGE WHEN BOTTLED	15 years
STRENGTH ABV	43%

TASTING NOTES	
NOSE	A delicious, full, fragrant bouquet of spirit, nuts and peat.
TASTE	Full bodied, fleshy, nutty and surprisingly refined. Finishes with an elegant sweetness.
COMMENTS	An outstanding after-dinner dram from the Chivas 'Heritage Selection'.

BRAND	**The Macallan**
	✉ Craigellachie, ABERLOUR, Banffshire AB38 9RX
	✆ 01340-871471
	🖷 01340-871212
MANAGER	David Robertson
OWNING COMPANY	The Macallan Distillers Ltd
PRODUCTION STATUS	Operational
ESTABLISHED	1824
SOURCE	Borehole aquifers
	🛢 Ex-sherry Spanish oak
	🥃 10
	🥃 5

㈗

🍃🦌📺

✆ 01340-871471

🖷 01340-871212

By appointment only. The restored Easter Elchies Jacobite manor is one of Speyside's unique whisky experiences.

AWARDS RECEIVED	Queen's Award for Exports (twice).
VISITORS PER YEAR	10,000

AGE WHEN BOTTLED	10, 18 & 25 years and 1977
STRENGTH ABV	10-y.o: 40%; all others: 43%
SPECIAL BOTTLINGS	1979, 18-y.o Gran Reserva @ 40%. 1946, 52-y.o @ 40%.
EXPORT BOTTLINGS	7, 10, 12, 18 & 25 years.

TASTING NOTES	10-year-old, 40%
NOSE	Smooth, sherry aroma – full of fragrance.
TASTE	Full-bodied, sherried with a long-lasting aftertaste of apples.
COMMENTS	One of the great Speysides. Highly popular. Expect to pay around £75 for the Gran Reserva and £1575 for the 1946.

RARE MALTS
SELECTION

Each individual vintage has been specially selected from Scotland's
finest single malt stocks of rare or now silent distilleries.
The limited bottlings of these scarce and unique whiskies are at
natural cask strength for the enjoyment of the true connoisseur.

NATURAL
CASK STRENGTH
SINGLE MALT
SCOTCH WHISKY

AGED **22** YEARS
DISTILLED 1974
MANNOCHMORE
DISTILLERY
ESTABLISHED 1971
BY ELGIN, MORAYSHIRE
60.1%vol 70cle
PRODUCED AND BOTTLED
IN SCOTLAND
LIMITED EDITION
BOTTLE
SEPTEMBER 1997 № 5362

BRAND	**Mannochmore**
✉	Birnie, ELGIN, Morayshire IV30 3SS
☎	01343-860331
🖷	01343-860302
MANAGER	Harry Fox
OWNING COMPANY	UDV
PRODUCTION STATUS	Operational
ESTABLISHED	1971
SOURCE	The Bardon Burn
🛢	Ex-bourbon
🍶	3
🍶	3

AGE WHEN BOTTLED	12 years
STRENGTH ABV	43%
SPECIAL BOTTLINGS	Loch Dhu, 10 years @ 40%. 22-y.o @ 60.1% Rare Malts Selection.

TASTING NOTES	12-year-old, 43%
NOSE	Fresh, light and aromatic with a dry sweetness and a faint smoky background.
TASTE	Delightful, fresh and stimulating, medium-dry creaminess which is both firm and balanced. Long-lasting sweet, dry finish.
COMMENTS	Another excellent all-round drink.

BRAND	**Miltonduff**
✉	ELGIN, Morayshire IV30 3TQ
☎	01343-547433
📠	01343-548802
MANAGER	John Black
OWNING COMPANY	Allied Distillers Ltd
PRODUCTION STATUS	Operational
ESTABLISHED	1824
SOURCE	Local springs and the Black Burn
🛢	Ex-bourbon
🍶	3
🍶	3

By appointment only.

AGE WHEN BOTTLED	12 years
STRENGTH ABV	40%
EXPORT BOTTLINGS	12 years

TASTING NOTES

NOSE — Agreeable, light, fragrant and aromatic bouquet.

TASTE — Medium-bodied with a pleasant, well-matured, subtle finish displaying a good balance of malt.

COMMENTS — After-dinner, but no longer available in the UK. Another malt called Mosstowie used to be produced from Lomond-type stills at Miltonduff and is available from the independent bottlers.

C A S K
STRENGTH

MORTLACH

SPEYSIDE SINGLE MALT
SCOTCH WHISKY

YEAR OF DISTILLATION
LIMITED 1980 TLING

BOTTLED IN 1997

63.1%vol   70cle

Distilled & Bottled in SCOTLAND
Mortlach Distillery, Dufftown, Keith, Banffshire, Scotland

THIS WONDERFULLY   DISTILLED IN 1980
COMPLEX SPEYSIDE MALT   THIS LIMITED BOTTLING,
HAS A RICH NOSE WITH   DIRECT FROM THE CASK, HAS
SUGGESTIONS OF SANDALWOOD THE NATURAL STRENGTH
AND ORANGES. BEST ENJOYED ACHIEVED AT MATURATION.
WITH THE ADDITION OF   BOTTLED IN 1997
WATER. ITS PERFECTLY
BALANCED FLAVOURS   BOTTLE NUMBER
GIVE WAY TO A LONG,   00278
LIQUORICE FILLED FINISH.

BRAND	**Mortlach**
✉	Dufftown, KEITH, Banffshire AB55 4AQ
☏	01340-820318
🖷	01340-820018
MANAGER	Steve McGingle
OWNING COMPANY	UDV
PRODUCTION STATUS	Operational
ESTABLISHED	c1823
SOURCE	Springs in the Conval Hills
🛢	Ex-bourbon
🍶	3
🍶	3

AGE WHEN BOTTLED	16 years
STRENGTH ABV	43%
SPECIAL BOTTLINGS	1980 @ 63.1%

TASTING NOTES

NOSE	Full, pleasant, well-rounded floral aroma with a touch of smoke. Refreshing.
TASTE	Rich and full with a hint of smoke and a pronounced sweetness which imparts a long, full, smooth, sherried finish.
COMMENTS	A first-class after-dinner malt also available for sale at the distillery office. See also pages 153-154.

SPEYSIDE
SINGLE MALT
SCOTCH WHISKY

PITTYVAICH

distillery is situated in the
DULLAN GLEN on the *outskirts*
of Dufftown, near to the *historic
Mortlach Church* which dates back
to the ()ᵗʰ The distillery draws
water from two nearby

springs - *CONVALLEYS* and
BALLIEMORE. Pittyvaich single
MALT SCOTCH WHISKY
has a *perfumed, fruity*
nose and a *robust* flavour with
a *hint of spiciness.*

AGED **12** YEARS

Distilled & Bottled in SCOTLAND
PITTYVAICH DISTILLERY
Dufftown, Keith, Banffshire, Scotland

43% vol 70 cl

BRAND	**Pittyvaich**
✉	Dufftown, KEITH, Banffshire AB55 4BR
☎	01340-820561/773
MANAGER	Steve McGingle
OWNING COMPANY	UDV
PRODUCTION STATUS	Operational
ESTABLISHED	1974
SOURCE	Two major local springs
🛢	Ex-bourbon
♨	2
♨	2

AGE WHEN BOTTLED	12 years
STRENGTH ABV	43%

TASTING NOTES

NOSE — Rather elegant with a delicate fragrance and a trace of smoke.

TASTE — Well-rounded, mellow and soft with a fruity palate.

COMMENTS — A remarkably good addition to the bottled malts. An after-dinner dram.

BRAND	**The Singleton of Auchroisk**
✉	MULBEN, Banffshire AB55 3XS
☎	01542-860333
🖷	01542-860265
MANAGER	Peter Warren
OWNING COMPANY	UDV
PRODUCTION STATUS	Operational
ESTABLISHED	1974
SOURCE	Dorie's Well
🛢	Predominantly ex-sherry
🥃	4
🥃	4
AWARDS RECEIVED	1995 IWSC: Gold Medal

AGE WHEN BOTTLED	10 years minimum, 12 for Japan
STRENGTH ABV	40%
EXPORT BOTTLINGS	43%

TASTING NOTES	1983, 40%
NOSE	Distinctive, rich, attractive bouquet with a touch of fruit and a tantalising suggestion of sherry.
TASTE	Medium-weight, hint of sherry sweetness and smoke with a delicious long-lasting flavour. Well-balanced – the sherry does not overpower the malt.
COMMENTS	After-dinner. A first-class malt international award-winning malt. The Singleton 'Particular' is available only in Japan.

BRAND	**Speyburn**
	✉ ROTHES, Morayshire IV33 7AG
	☎ 01340-831213
	📠 01340-831678
MANAGER	Graham MacWilliam
OWNING COMPANY	Inver House Distillers Ltd
PRODUCTION STATUS	Operational
ESTABLISHED	1897
SOURCE	The Granty Burn sourced on the western slope of the Glen of Rothes
🛢	Ex-bourbon
🍶	1
🍶	1

AGE WHEN BOTTLED	10 years
STRENGTH ABV	40%

TASTING NOTES	
NOSE	A heather-honey bouquet with overtones of peat.
TASTE	Big, full-bodied malty taste with a sweet, honey and aromatic finish.
COMMENTS	After-dinner and now widely available under its new owners.

"STRATHISLA"
PURE HIGHLAND MALT
SCOTCH WHISKY
THE OLDEST DISTILLERY IN THE HIGHLANDS
AGED **12** YEARS

BRAND	**Strathisla**
	(Strath-eyela)
⊠	KEITH, Banffshire AB55 3BS
☏	01542-783044
🖷	01542-783055
MANAGER	Norman Green
OWNING COMPANY	Chivas Brothers
PRODUCTION STATUS	Operational
ESTABLISHED	1786
SOURCE	Fons Bulliens's Well
🛢	Ex-bourbon
🔥	2
🔥	2

🚻	🚻🔲
☏	01542-783044
🖷	01542-783039
	Feb to mid-Mar, Mon-Fri: 09.30-16.00. Mid-Mar to end Nov, Mon-Sat: 09.30-16.30. Sun: 12.30-16.00. £4 entry charge, part-redeemable in shop for whisky. Under eights not admitted to production areas.
OTHER ATTRACTIONS	Free coffee and shortbread, visitor handbook. Nosings.
AWARDS RECEIVED	1995 IWSC: Bronze Medal. 1996 IWSC: Silver Medal.

AGE WHEN BOTTLED	12 years
STRENGTH ABV	43%

TASTING NOTES	
NOSE	Beautiful, bewitching fragrance of fruit which also reflects the taste to come.
TASTE	Slender hint of fruit with a light sweetness and an extremely long, lingering fullness. Good balance.
COMMENTS	An excellent after-dinner malt and one of the best to sip and savour. A Chivas 'Heritage Selection' malt.

BRAND	**Tamdhu**
	(Tamm-doo)
✉	Knockando, ABERLOUR, Morayshire AB38 7RP
☎	01340-871471
🖷	01340-872144
MANAGER	Dr W. Crilly
OWNING COMPANY	Highland Distillers
PRODUCTION STATUS	Operational
ESTABLISHED	1896-7
SOURCE	A spring beneath the distillery
🛢	Ex-bourbon and sherry
⚗	Saladin maltings
🍶	3
🍶	3

TASTING NOTES	10-year-old, 40%
NOSE	Light aroma with a trace of honey sweetness.
TASTE	Medium, with a little fruity sweetness and a very mellow finish.
COMMENTS	A good after-dinner dram which is both popular and readily available. No age statement given.

BRAND	**Tamnavulin**
	(Tamna-voolin)
✉	BALLINDALLOCH, Banffshire AB37 9JA
☎	01807-590285
🖶	01807-590342
MANAGER	Robert Fleming
OWNING COMPANY	Jim Beam Brands (Greater Europe) plc
PRODUCTION STATUS	Mothballed, 1995
ESTABLISHED	1965-6
SOURCE	Underground reservoir fed by springs
🛢	American white oak
⚗ 3	
⚗ 3	

⑭	🚻 ♿ ▣ ♿
☎	01807-590442
	Apr to Oct, Mon-Sat: 09.30-16.30. Oct, Mon-Fri:
	09.30-16.30. July & Aug, Sun: 12.30-16.30.
OTHER ATTRACTIONS	Coffee shop.
VISITORS PER YEAR	10,000

AGE WHEN BOTTLED	12 years
STRENGTH ABV	40%
SPECIAL BOTTLINGS	Stillman's Dram: 25 years
EXPORT BOTTLINGS	43%

TASTING NOTES	12-year-old, 40%
NOSE	Well-matured with a distinct mellowness and a hint of floral sweetness.
TASTE	Medium weight with a light, smoky, long, pronounced finish.
COMMENTS	A good all-round malt.

BRAND	**Tomintoul**
	(Tommin-towl)
✉	BALLINDALLOCH, Banffshire AB37 9AQ
☏	01807-590274
🖷	01807-590342
MANAGER	Robert Fleming
OWNING COMPANY	Jim Beam Brands (Greater Europe) plc
PRODUCTION STATUS	Operational
ESTABLISHED	1964-5
SOURCE	The Ballantruan Spring
🛢	American white oak, oloroso sherry butts
🍶	2
🍶	2

🏠

By appointment only. Group bookings limited to 10.

AGE WHEN BOTTLED	10 years
STRENGTH ABV	40%
EXPORT BOTTLINGS	43%

TASTING NOTES	12-year-old, 43%
NOSE	Light and delicate.
TASTE	Light body with good character.
COMMENTS	A good introduction to malt, but only to be found in Oddbins.

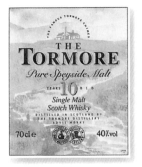

BRAND	**The Tormore**
✉	Advie, GRANTOWN-ON-SPEY, Morayshire PH26 3LR
☎	01807-510244
📠	01807-510352
MANAGER	Ronnie MacDonald
OWNING COMPANY	Allied Distillers Ltd
PRODUCTION STATUS	Operational
ESTABLISHED	1960
SOURCE	The Achvochkie Burn
🍶	4
🍶	4

🏛

By appointment only. Telephone in advance.

AGE WHEN BOTTLED	10 years
STRENGTH ABV	40%
EXPORT BOTTLINGS	43%

TASTING NOTES

NOSE	Well-defined dry aroma.
TASTE	Medium-bodied with a hint of sweetness and a pleasant, lingering aftertaste.
COMMENTS	After-dinner. No longer available in the UK.

The Highlands

THE core of distilling in the Highlands is obviously Speyside, but it is surrounded with distilling activity on all points of the compass – in the North, South, East and West. Changes in ownership have occurred here too with Royal Brackla going to William Lawson (subject to EU approval) and Pulteney now with Inver House. It is good to see Old Pulteney back on the market as a vibrant brand. These developments are set against the background of defunct plants that have passed into the history books. Although over 30 malts emanate from the Highlands, six are from distilleries no longer in existence. These are Glen Mhor, Glen Albyn and Millburn in Inverness, Banff (at the town of the same name), Glenugie near Peterhead and North Port in Brechin. Some other distilleries are closed with only vestiges of them still remaining; these will never open again and include Glenury-Royal in Stonehaven, Coleburn near Elgin, Glenlochy in Fort William, Brora in the town of that name and Glenesk (formerly North Esk or Hillside) in Montrose. Details on these and other malts are in the chapter Lost Distilleries on page 133.

The existing distilling activity in the Northern Highlands stretches from Kingussie to Wick in the north, and encompasses Tomatin, Royal Brackla near Nairn; Ord Distillery at Muir of Ord in the Black Isle; Dalmore and Teaninich at Alness; Balblair and Glenmorangie near Tain and Clynelish near Brora.

The Eastern malts lie between the Speyside region and the North Sea coast. Banff, the fishing town on the Moray Firth now only possesses one distillery, Glen Deveron. Glen Garioch Distillery at Oldmeldrum in Aberdeenshire is operational once more and Royal Lochnagar is still catering for thousands of visitors seeking the delights of Royal Deeside. To the south-east Old Fettercairn extends the activity to Montrose, which used to boast a considerable amount of distilling. The Glenesk Distillery will not produce again and Lochside Distillery (a converted brewery) which once produced both grain and malt whisky, is now closed with no prospect of reopening.

Further inland, but still on the South Esk river, Brechin has one producing distillery at Glencadam and a defunct one at North Port – both of them quite rare malts. South of this arable region the hills of Perthshire signal the southern limits of the Highland distilling area.

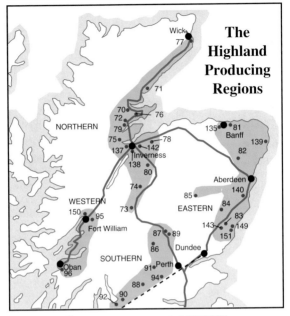

The Highland Producing Regions

DISTILLERY LOCATION NUMBERS REFER TO PAGE NUMBERS

At Pitlochry the enthusiast can experience two contrasting distilleries. Edradour is the smallest in Scotland and yet maintains all the advantages of a small 19th-century plant, while Blair Athol is a large, relatively modern distillery. Aberfeldy Distillery (changing hands to Bacardi) lies at the eastern entrance to the town of the same name on the banks of the River Tay and Glenturret Distillery at Crieff lies in a very picturesque location. Tullibardine at Blackford is a 'recent' distillery (1948) in a village which not only produces bottled mineral water (Highland Spring) but also has the only commercial malting floors in Scotland built on arguably the oldest brewery site in Scotland! And if that amount of diversity is a surprise, Deanston Distillery on the River Teith at Doune, near Stirling, is a converted cotton mill where the vaulted weaving sheds act as bonded warehouses. A small hydro-electric generating station is also situated within the plant itself and a gin distillery has just been brought on stream here!

In the west of this most southerly of the Highland regions lie Loch Lomond and Glengoyne distilleries. Both almost straddle the Highland line (as does Tullibardine) but claim allegiance to the Highland region. Loch Lomond, built in 1968, produces both Inchmurrin and Old Rhosdhu malts from stills that can facilitate this curious diversity of operation. The owning company also owns

Glen Scotia in Campbeltown and Littlemill at Bowling. Glengoyne has a longer pedigree and, resting in a cleft of the Campsie Fells, is a unique distillery in a unique setting.

The Western malts, although only three in number, have suffered only one loss. Glenlochy in Fort William will never produce again, but Oban Distillery, situated just off the High Street of this thriving tourist town, is extremely accessible for the visitor and is one of United Distillers' Classic Malts. Ben Nevis Distillery in Fort William is also prospering and continues to draw visitors off the 'Road to the Isles' for the 'Dew of Ben Nevis' experience.

Thought For Food

In the Northern Highlands there are several malts with a certain sweet spiciness and heathery character. A more fruity style can be found in the more sheltered Eastern Highlands and Perthshire while in the west there are definite mild salty and peat sensations. This diversity across the region lends itself ideally to the cheeseboard and charcuteries.

Dalwhinnie 15-year-old and Caboc.

Edradour 10-year-old and Cumbria mature royal ham (air dried).

Oban 14-year-old with smoked cheddar and oatcakes.

NORTHERN HIGHLANDS

BRAND	**Balblair**
	✉ Edderton, TAIN, Ross-shire IV19 1LB
	☏ 01862-821273
	🖷 01862-821360
MANAGER	Derick Sinclair
OWNING COMPANY	Allied Distillers Ltd
PRODUCTION STATUS	Mothballed 1996
ESTABLISHED	1790
SOURCE	Struie Hill
🛢	Ex-bourbon
⚗	1
⚗	1
VISITORS PER YEAR	800

AGE WHEN BOTTLED	5, 10 years
STRENGTH ABV	40%

TASTING NOTES	10-year-old
NOSE	Pronounced, distinctive, aromatic fragrance of smoke and sweetness.
TASTE	Good lingering flavour, long-lasting with a slender hint of sweetness.
COMMENTS	A fine dram at any time. Bottled by Ballantines.

BRAND	**Clynelish**
	(Kline-leesh)
✉	BRORA, Sutherland KW9 6LR
☎	01408-623000
🖷	01408-623004
MANAGER	Bob Robertson
OWNING COMPANY	UDV
PRODUCTION STATUS	Operational
ESTABLISHED	1819, new distillery built in 1967.
SOURCE	Clynemilton Burn
🛢	Ex-bourbon
🥃	3
🥃	3

(🏭)	🏭 🖥 ♿
☎	01408-623014
🖷	01408-623016
	Mar to Oct, Mon-Fri: 09.30-16.00. Nov to Feb, by appointment only.
AWARDS RECEIVED	Gold Award for Safety (ROSPA)
VISITORS PER YEAR	12,000

AGE WHEN BOTTLED	14 years
STRENGTH ABV	43%
SPECIAL BOTTLINGS	24-y.o @ 61.3% Rare Malts Selection

TASTING NOTES	14-year-old , 43%
NOSE	Peaty for a Northern malt with a soft hint of sweet fruit.
TASTE	Full, pleasant palate with a slightly dry finish. Lots of character, retaining a full flavour of fruit.
COMMENTS	Fine after-dinner drinking.

BRAND	**The Dalmore**
✉	ALNESS, Ross-shire IV17 0UT
☎	01349-882362
🖷	01349-883655
MANAGER	Steve Tulewicz
OWNING COMPANY	Jim Beam Brands (Greater Europe) plc
PRODUCTION STATUS	Operational
ESTABLISHED	c1839
SOURCE	Gildermory loch
🛢	American white oak, oloroso sherry butts
🍾	4
🍶	4

🏛

By appointment only. Groups limited to a maximum of 10.

AGE WHEN BOTTLED	12 years
STRENGTH ABV	40%
SPECIAL BOTTLINGS	Stillman's Dram, 26-year-old
EXPORT BOTTLINGS	43%

TASTING NOTES	
NOSE	Rich, fresh, with a suggestion of sweetness.
TASTE	Full of honey flavour which finishes a touch dry despite the sherry influence. Wonderfully balanced.
COMMENTS	Another really good malt. After-dinner.

BRAND	**Dalwhinnie**
✉	DALWHINNIE, Inverness-shire PH19 1AB
☏	01528-522264
🖶	01528-522240
MANAGER	Robert Christine
OWNING COMPANY	UDV
PRODUCTION STATUS	Operational
ESTABLISHED	1898
SOURCE	Allt an t'Sluie Burn
🛢	Ex-bourbon
⚗	1
⚗	1

(H)	
	⚏🍸♿
☏	01528-522208
🖶	01528-522296
	Mar to Dec, Mon-Fri: 09.30-16.30. June to Oct, Mon-Sat: 09.30-16.30. July & Aug, Mon-Sun: 12.30-16.30. Jan to Mar, restricted hours, please telephone.
VISITORS PER YEAR	40,000

AGE WHEN BOTTLED	15 years
STRENGTH ABV	43%
SPECIAL BOTTLINGS	Distiller's Edition, 1980

TASTING NOTES	
NOSE	A gentle, aromatic bouquet of freshly cut flowers.
TASTE	Luscious flavour with a light, honey-sweet, crisp finish.
COMMENTS	Pre-dinner dramming of the highest quality.

BRAND	**Drumguish**
	(Drum-yewish)
✉	Tromie Mills, KINGUSSIE, Inverness-shire PH21 1NS
☎	01540-661060
🖷	01540-661959
MANAGER	Richard Beattie
OWNING COMPANY	Speyside Distillery Co Ltd
PRODUCTION STATUS	Operational
ESTABLISHED	1990
SOURCE	River Tromie
🛢	Ex-sherry hogsheads
🍶	1
🍶	1
OTHER ATTRACTIONS	Borders a wildlife sanctuary.

AGE WHEN BOTTLED	No age given
STRENGTH ABV	40%

TASTING NOTES	
NOSE	Pleasant, malty aroma with a delicate hint of sweetness and apple blossom.
TASTE	Very smooth, delicate sweetness importing fruitiness to the palate. Well-balanced with a lingering, gentle finish.
COMMENTS	A welcome addition to Scotland's malt portfolio.

BRAND	**Glen Ord**
✉	MUIR OF ORD, Ross-shire IV6 7UJ
☎	01463-870421
🖷	01463-872002
MANAGER	Kenny Gray
OWNING COMPANY	UDV
PRODUCTION STATUS	Operational
ESTABLISHED	1838
SOURCE	Lochs Nan Eun and Nam Bonnach
🛢	Ex-bourbon
⌂	Associated industrial maltings
🝆	3
🝆	3

🕉

🎁📷♿

☎ 01463-872004

🖷 01463-872008

Jan to Nov, Mon-Fri, 09.30-16.30. July to Aug, Sat: 09.30-16.30, Sun: 12.00-16.30. Dec: by appointment.

OTHER ATTRACTIONS	STB commended exhibition.
AWARDS RECEIVED	1996 Grand Gold Medal, Monde Selection
VISITORS PER YEAR	27,000

AGE WHEN BOTTLED	12 years
STRENGTH ABV	40%
SPECIAL BOTTLINGS	23-y.o @ 59.8% Rare Malts Selection

TASTING NOTES	
NOSE	A beautifully deep nose with a tinge of dryness and mixed spice.
TASTE	Good depth with a long-lasting, delicious aftertaste. Very smooth and rather moreish.
COMMENTS	After-dinner with a growing reputation. Much in evidence in Melrose on the second Saturday in April!

BRAND	**Glenmorangie**
✉	TAIN, Ross-shire IV19 1PZ
☏	01862-892043
🖷	01862-893862
MANAGER	Dr Bill Lumsden
OWNING COMPANY	Glenmorangie plc
PRODUCTION STATUS	Operational
ESTABLISHED	1843
SOURCE	Tarlogie Springs
🛢	Ex-bourbon, port, sherry and madeira wood
🍾	4
🥃	4

(ıɖı)

🏛♥■🗠

☏ 01862-892477

Visitors are welcome. Phone in advance.

OTHER ATTRACTIONS	Recently opened museum.
VISITORS PER YEAR	8,000

AGE WHEN BOTTLED	10, 18 years
STRENGTH ABV	40%, 43% and cask strength
SPECIAL BOTTLINGS	Port, sherry and Madeira wood finishes

TASTING NOTES	10-year-old, 40%
NOSE	Beautiful aroma. Fresh and sweet with a subtle hint of peat.
TASTE	Medium-bodied with a sweet, fresh, satisfying finish. One to linger and dwell upon.
COMMENTS	An excellent malt, very popular. Entire distillery output is sold as single, bottled malt.

BRAND	**Old Pulteney**
	(Pult-nay)
✉	Huddart Street, WICK, Caithness KW1 5BA
☎	01955-602371
📠	01955-602279
MANAGER	Donald Raitt
OWNING COMPANY	Inver House Distillers Ltd
PRODUCTION STATUS	Operational
ESTABLISHED	1826
SOURCE	Mains water
🛢	Ex-bourbon and sherry
🕯	1
🕯	1

AGE WHEN BOTTLED	12, 15 years
STRENGTH ABV	40%, 15-y.o: 60.6%

TASTING NOTES	12-year-old, 40%
NOSE	Fine, delicate, light aroma with a hint of the island malts.
TASTE	Light, crisp and refreshing with a hint of fullness which gives a positive, smoky finish.
COMMENTS	An excellent aperitif whisky from the most northerly mainland distillery in Scotland. A welcome return under new ownership.

BRAND	**Royal Brackla**
	✉ Cawdor, NAIRN, Nairnshire IV12 5QY
	☎ 01667-404280
	📠 01667-404743
MANAGER	Chris Anderson
OWNING COMPANY	William Lawson Distillers Ltd
PRODUCTION STATUS	Operational
ESTABLISHED	c1812
SOURCE	The Cawdor Burn
	🛢 Ex-bourbon
	🥃 2
	🥃 2

AGE WHEN BOTTLED	10 years
STRENGTH ABV	43%
SPECIAL BOTTLINGS	No age given, 40%

TASTING NOTES	No age given, 40%
NOSE	Refreshing aroma of peat smoke with a delicate hint of sweetness and a floral overtone.
TASTE	Round, medium-sweet with a fullness which becomes dry on the palate but then has a lingering, tender sweetness which is almost sherry-like.
COMMENTS	Excellent and refreshing.

Each individual vintage has been specially selected from Scotland's
finest single malt stocks of rare or now silent distilleries.
The limited bottlings of these scarce and unique whiskies are at
natural cask strength for the enjoyment of the true connoisseur.

NATURAL CASK STRENGTH
SINGLE MALT
SCOTCH WHISKY

AGED **23** YEARS

DISTILLED 1973
TEANINICH
DISTILLERY
ESTABLISHED 1817
ALNESS, ROSS-SHIRE

57.1%vol 70cle
PRODUCED AND BOTTLED
IN SCOTLAND
LIMITED EDITION
BOTTLE No 3596
APRIL 1997

BRAND		**Teaninich**
	✉	ALNESS, Ross-shire IV17 0XB
	☏	01349-882461
	🖷	01349-883864
MANAGER		Angus Paul
OWNING COMPANY		UDV
PRODUCTION STATUS		Operational
ESTABLISHED		1817
SOURCE		The Dairywell Spring
	🍶	3
	🍶	3

AGE WHEN BOTTLED	10 years
STRENGTH ABV	43%
SPECIAL BOTTLINGS	1973 @ 57.1% Rare Malts Selection

TASTING NOTES	
NOSE	Fresh, light touch of smoke with a hint of fruit and a delicate sweetness.
TASTE	Medium balance with a gentle oakiness and a smooth, long finish. Well balanced.
COMMENTS	An excellent all-rounder.

BRAND	**Tomatin**
	(Tommaa-tin)
✉	TOMATIN, Inverness-shire IV13 7YT
☎	01808-511444
🖷	01808-511373
MANAGER	Tom McCulloch
OWNING COMPANY	Tomatin Distillery Co Ltd
PRODUCTION STATUS	Operational
ESTABLISHED	1897
SOURCE	Allt na Frithe Burn
🛢	Ex-bourbon
🕯 12
🕯 11

🏭	🚻♿🖵♿
☎	01808-511444
🖷	01808-511373
	Mon-Fri: 09.00-17.00, last tour at 15.30. May to Oct, Sat: 09.00-13.00, last tour at 12.00. Group bookings by appointment.
VISITORS PER YEAR	70,000

AGE WHEN BOTTLED	10 years
STRENGTH ABV	40%
EXPORT BOTTLINGS	10, 12 years, 40 & 43%

TASTING NOTES	
NOSE	Pleasant and light. Delicate touch of sweetness, subtly smoky.
TASTE	Light body, very smooth and rounded with a gentle length of finish.
COMMENTS	A good pre-dinner dram. This huge distillery was the first to be acquired by the Japanese in 1985.

EASTERN HIGHLANDS

BRAND	**Glen Deveron**
✉	BANFF, Banffshire AB4 3JT
☎	01261-812612
🖷	01261-818083
MANAGER	Michael Roy
OWNING COMPANY	William Lawson Distillers Ltd
PRODUCTION STATUS	Operational
ESTABLISHED	1960
SOURCE	Local spring
🛢	Ex-bourbon
🍶	2
🍶	3
AWARDS RECEIVED	1993/4 IWSC: Silver Medal

AGE WHEN BOTTLED	12 years
STRENGTH ABV	40%
EXPORT BOTTLINGS	5, 10 & 12 years @ 40 & 43%

TASTING NOTES	
NOSE	Assertive, refreshing bouquet.
TASTE	Medium-weight. Smooth, pleasant, slightly sweet flavour with a clean finish.
COMMENTS	An after-dinner dram which is also available as Macduff from the independent bottlers. See pages 153-154.

BRAND	**Glen Garioch**
	(Glen Geery)
✉	Oldmeldrum, Aberdeenshire AB51 0ES
☎	01651-872706
🖷	01651-872578
MANAGER	Fraser Hughes
OWNING COMPANY	Morrison Bowmore Distillers Ltd
PRODUCTION STATUS	Operational
ESTABLISHED	1797
SOURCE	Springs on Percock Hill
🛢	Ex-bourbon and sherry
♨	Floor maltings
🍶	2
🍶	2

AGE WHEN BOTTLED	8, 15 & 21 years
STRENGTH ABV	8-y.o: 40%; 15 & 21-y.o: 43%
SPECIAL BOTTLINGS	21-y.o. Ceramics (Red, Blue & Green) @ 43%

TASTING NOTES	21-year-old, 43%
NOSE	Delicate and smoky. Hints of sweetness.
TASTE	Pronounced, peaty flavour with a smooth, rich and pleasant finish.
COMMENTS	A good after-dinner dram.

Vintage 1980
Single Malt Scotch Whisky

Matured in sherry casks for 15 years
Distilled at Glencadam Distillery
on 17.10.80   Bottled 10.95
Batt no. 6375   Bottle no.   of 654
This whisky has been selected, produced and bottled in
Scotland for and under the sole responsibility of
Signatory Vintage Scotch Whisky Co. Ltd.
Edinburgh EH6 6LU
70cl   43%vol

MALT	**Glencadam**
✉	BRECHIN, Angus DD9 7PA
☎	01356-622217
🖷	01356-624926
MANAGER	Calcott Innes Harper
OWNING COMPANY	Allied Distillers Ltd
PRODUCTION STATUS	Operational
ESTABLISHED	1825
SOURCE	Loch Lee
🛢	Ex-bourbon
♠	1
♠	1

🏚

	Sept to June, Mon-Thu: 14.00-16.00. Group bookings maximum 10. All visits by appointment.
OTHER ATTRACTIONS	Nature trail, public park.
VISITORS PER YEAR	400

TASTING NOTES	1974, 40%
NOSE	Light, sweet and soft.
TASTE	Full, with quite a fruity flavour and some smoke on the back of the palate. A good finish.
COMMENTS	An after-dinner malt. See pages 153-154.

BRAND	**Old Fettercairn**
✉	Distillery Road, LAURENCEKIRK, Kincardineshire AB30 1YE
☎	01561-340244
🖶	01561-340447
MANAGER	Bernie Kenny
OWNING COMPANY	Jim Beam Brands (Greater Europe) plc
PRODUCTION STATUS	Operational
ESTABLISHED	c1824
SOURCE	Springs in the Grampian Mountains
🛢	American white oak, oloroso sherry butts
🍶	2
🍶	2

🏭

🚻 ♿ 🥃

☎ 01561-340244

May to Sept, Mon-Sat: 10.00-16.30. Groups by appointment.

VISITORS PER YEAR	10,000

AGE WHEN BOTTLED	10 years
STRENGTH ABV	40%
EXPORT BOTTLINGS	43%

TASTING NOTES

NOSE	Light, stimulating, fresh aroma with a hint of dry malt.
TASTE	Fresh, slightly dry, nutty finish which is quite stimulating.
COMMENTS	A good all-round malt. Reputedly the second 'legal' distillery after the 1823 legislation.

BRAND	**Royal Lochnagar**
	✉ Crathie, BALLATER, Aberdeenshire AB35 5TB
	☎ 01339-742273
	🖷 01339-742312
MANAGER	Alastair Skakles
OWNING COMPANY	UDV
PRODUCTION STATUS	Operational
ESTABLISHED	1845
SOURCE	Local springs below Lochnagar
🛢	Ex-bourbon and sherry
⚗	1
⚗	1

(H)

⚓🚻◻♿

☎ 01339-742273

🖷 01339-742312

All year: Mon-Fri: 10.00-17.00. Easter to Oct, Sat: 10.00-17.00. Sun: 11.00-16.00. Groups by appointment. Admission charge redeemable in shop.

OTHER ATTRACTIONS	Balmoral Castle.
VISITORS PER YEAR	35,000

AGE WHEN BOTTLED	12 years and no age given
STRENGTH ABV	40 and 43%
SPECIAL BOTTLINGS	23-y.o @ 59.7% & 24-y.o @ 55.7% Rare Malts Selection

TASTING NOTES	12-year-old, 40%
NOSE	Pleasant, full rich fruity aroma.
TASTE	Good body with a full, malty, fruity taste and a delicious, creamy trace of sweetness.
COMMENTS	Also available as Selected Reserve at around £175 per bottle.

SOUTHERN HIGHLANDS

BRAND	**Aberfeldy**
✉	ABERFELDY, Perthshire PH15 2EB
☎	01887-820330
📠	01887-822003
MANAGER	Gordon Donoghue
OWNING COMPANY	William Lawson Distillers Ltd
PRODUCTION STATUS	Operational
ESTABLISHED	1898
SOURCE	Pitillie Burn
🛢	Ex-bourbon and sherry
♨	2
♨	2

🏭	
	♿ 🚻
☎	01887-820330
📠	01887-820432
	Easter to Oct, Mon-Fri: 10.00-16.00. Dec to Feb: by appointment only. Admission charge redeemable in shop.
OTHER ATTRACTIONS	Nature trail.
VISITORS PER YEAR	10,000

AGE WHEN BOTTLED	15 years
STRENGTH ABV	43%
SPECIAL BOTTLINGS	1980 @ 62.0%

TASTING NOTES	
NOSE	Fresh, clean, sherry overtones with hints of walnut. Lightly peated.
TASTE	Substantial flavour with a rich sweetness and a hint of smoke. Well-rounded.
COMMENTS	Increasingly popular.

BRAND	**Blair Athol**
	✉ PITLOCHRY, Perthshire PH16 5LY
	☏ 01796-472161
	🖷 01796-473292
MANAGER	Gordon Donoghue
OWNING COMPANY	UDV
PRODUCTION STATUS	Operational
ESTABLISHED	1798
SOURCE	Allt Dour
	🛢 Ex-bourbon
	🍶 2
	🍶 2

(ⱷ)

⚒ ♥ 🖥 ♿

☏ 01796-472234

🖷 01796-473292

All year, Mon-Fri: 09.30-17.00. Easter to Oct, Mon-Sat: 09.30-17.00. Sun: 12.00-17.00. Last tours at 16.00 in Summer and 15.30 in Winter. Groups by appointment only. Admission charge redeemable in shop.

VISITORS PER YEAR	50,000

AGE WHEN BOTTLED	12 years
STRENGTH ABV	43%
SPECIAL BOTTLINGS	1981 @ 55.5%

TASTING NOTES	
NOSE	Light, fresh and clean with hints of citrus.
TASTE	Medium hint of peat and sweetness with a rounded finish. Plenty of lingering flavour.
COMMENTS	Pre-dinner drinking from one of Scotland's oldest distilleries.

BUILT IN 1745

DEANSTON
Single
Malt Scotch Whisky

From the DEANSTON DISTILLERY
originally built as a mill in 1785 on the
pure soft waters of the historic
RIVER TEITH near Castle Doune Perthshire

OVER **12** YEARS

A fine mellow Single HIGHLAND
MALT with a fragrant fruity
flavour, and a lingering sweet
after taste.

PRODUCT OF SCOTLAND

BRAND	**Deanston**
✉	DOUNE, Perthshire FK16 6AG
☎	01786-841422
🖷	01786-841439
MANAGER	Ian Macmillan
OWNING COMPANY	Burn Stewart Distillers plc
PRODUCTION STATUS	Operational
ESTABLISHED	1965-6, on the site of a cotton mill, est c1785
SOURCE	River Teith
🛢	American and Spanish oak hogsheads and butts, some fresh sherry butts.
♨	2
♨	2

🏭	♿
	Trade visitors only.
OTHER ATTRACTIONS	Doune Castle is nearby.

AGE WHEN BOTTLED	12 years, 17 & 25 years
STRENGTH ABV	40%
SPECIAL BOTTLINGS	25-y.o vintage

TASTING NOTES	12-year-old
NOSE	Fresh, light hint of sweetness with a slightly dry, nasal effect and hints of fruit and malt.
TASTE	Medium-sweet, light, honeyed and smooth with an attractive, long, finish.
COMMENTS	A very refreshing and stimulating dram from a distillery situated beside a fine salmon river.

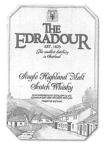

BRAND	**The Edradour**
	(Eddra-dower)
✉	PITLOCHRY, Perthshire PH16 5JP
☎	01786-473524
🖷	01786-472002
MANAGER	John Reid
OWNING COMPANY	Campbell Distillers Ltd
PRODUCTION STATUS	Operational
ESTABLISHED	1825
SOURCE	Local springs on Moulin Moor
🛢	Ex-bourbon
⚗	1
⚗	1

🏭	⚐♥▬🦽
☎	01796-472095
🖷	01796-472002
	Mar to Oct, Mon-Sat: 09.30-17.00. Sun: 12.00-17.00.
	Nov to Feb, Mon-Sat: 10.00-16.00, shop only. Groups
	over 14 by appointment only.
VISITORS PER YEAR	100,000

AGE WHEN BOTTLED	10 years
STRENGTH ABV	40%
EXPORT BOTTLINGS	43%

TASTING NOTES	
NOSE	Fruity-sweet, smoky and lightly aromatic.
TASTE	Light marzipan which comes through smoothly. Slightly dry and malty with a nutty, almond-like aftertaste. Wonderful balance.
COMMENTS	Excellent malt from Scotland's smallest Victorian distillery.

BRAND	**Glengoyne**
✉	DUMGOYNE, Stirlingshire G63 9LB
☎	01360-550229
📠	01360-550094
MANAGER	Sandy Lawtie
OWNING COMPANY	Lang Brothers Ltd
PRODUCTION STATUS	Operational
ESTABLISHED	c1833
SOURCE	Distillery Burn from the Campsie Hills
🍶	Refill whisky and ex-sherry oak
🥃	1
🥃	2

🏚

    📠♥️▢♿

☎ 01360-550254

📠 01360-550094

All year, hourly tours. Mon-Sat: 10.00-16.00. Easter to Nov, Sun: 12.00-16.00. Groups over 10 by appointment only. Admission charge £3. Closed Dec 25 and Jan 1.

OTHER ATTRACTIONS	ASVA recommended. Evening functions can be booked.
VISITORS PER YEAR	40,000

AGE WHEN BOTTLED	10, 17, 21 & 30 years
STRENGTH ABV	10-y.o: 40%; 17 & 21-y.o: 43%
SPECIAL BOTTLINGS	Occasional vintages
EXPORT BOTTLINGS	10, 17 & 21-y.o. @ 43%. USA: Reserve @ 52.5%, distilled Nov 27, 1967.

TASTING NOTES	17-year-old
NOSE	Refreshing, rich, oak and fruit aroma with a creamy toffee overtone.
TASTE	Soft, smooth with warm hints of vanilla and a long, mellow finish.
COMMENTS	Unpeated malt makes for impressive whisky.

BRAND		**The Glenturret**
	✉	The Hosh, CRIEFF, Perthshire PH7 4HA
	☎	01764-656565
	📠	01764-654366
MANAGER		Neil Cameron
OWNING COMPANY		Highland Distillers
PRODUCTION STATUS		Operational
ESTABLISHED		1775
SOURCE		Loch Turret
	🛢	Refill whisky and ex-sherry oak
	🛢	1
	🛢	1

🏠		⚑♥◼♿
	☎	01764-656565
	📠	01764-654366
		Open all year. Water of Life audio-visual, Spirit of the Glen Exhibition, Pagoda and Kiln rooms. Director of Tourism: Derek Brown.
OTHER ATTRACTIONS		Smuggler's Restaurant.
AWARDS RECEIVED		1974/81/91 IWSC: Gold Medal
VISITORS PER YEAR		228,416

AGE WHEN BOTTLED	12, 15 & 18 years
STRENGTH ABV	40%; 15-y.o: 50%
SPECIAL BOTTLINGS	1966 @ 40% (27-y.o.)
EXPORT BOTTLINGS	12 years & Malt Liqueur

TASTING NOTES	12-year-old
NOSE	Very impressive aromatic nose. Delicate and sweet.
TASTE	Full, lush body with good depth of flavour and a stimulating finish.
COMMENTS	Consistently fine spirit from arguably Scotland's oldest distillery.

BRAND	**Inchmurrin**
DISTILLERY	Loch Lomond
✉	ALEXANDRIA, Dunbartonshire G83 0TL
☎	01389-752781
📠	01389-757977
MANAGER	J. Peterson
OWNING COMPANY	Loch Lomond Distillery Co Ltd
PRODUCTION STATUS	Operational
ESTABLISHED	1966
SOURCE	Loch Lomond
🛢	Ex-bourbon
⚗	2
⚗	2

AGE WHEN BOTTLED	10 years
STRENGTH ABV	40%

TASTING NOTES

NOSE	Slightly aromatic. Follows through on the palate with a subtle dryness.
TASTE	Light-bodied, slight promise of sweetness. Most of the flavour is on the front of the palate and thus finishes quickly.
COMMENTS	An everyday drinking malt.

BRAND	**Old Rhosdhu**
DISTILLERY	Loch Lomond
✉	ALEXANDRIA, Dunbartonshire G83 0TL
☏	01389-752781
🖶	01389-757977
MANAGER	J. Peterson
OWNING COMPANY	Loch Lomond Distillery Co Ltd
PRODUCTION STATUS	Operational
ESTABLISHED	1966
SOURCE	Loch Lomond
🛢	Ex-bourbon
🥃	2
🥃	2

AGE WHEN BOTTLED	5 years
STRENGTH ABV	40%

TASTING NOTES	
NOSE	Aromatic, rich, malty and sweet.
TASTE	Light-bodied, sweet and clean. Most of the flavour and taste is on the front of the palate and therefore does not linger.
COMMENTS	An dram for drinking at any time.

BRAND	**Tullibardine**
	(Tully-bardeen)
✉	Blackford, AUCHTERARDER, Perthshire PH4 1QG
☎	01764-682252
OWNING COMPANY	Jim Beam Brands (Greater Europe) plc
PRODUCTION STATUS	Non-operational
ESTABLISHED	1949
SOURCE	The Ochil Hills
🛢	American white oak
♨	2
♨	2

AGE WHEN BOTTLED	10 years
STRENGTH ABV	40%
SPECIAL BOTTLINGS	25-year old Stillman's Dram occasionally available.
EXPORT BOTTLINGS	43%

TASTING NOTES	
NOSE	Delicate, mellow, sweet aroma of fruit.
TASTE	Full bodied, with a fruity flavour and a lingering finish of sweet malt.
COMMENTS	A pre-dinner dram from another distillery designed by W. Delmé-Evans.

WESTERN HIGHLANDS

BRAND	**Ben Nevis**
✉	FORT WILLIAM, Inverness-shire PH33 6TJ
☏	01397-702476
🖶	01397-702768
MANAGER	Colin Ross
OWNING COMPANY	Ben Nevis Distillery (Fort William) Ltd
PRODUCTION STATUS	Operational
ESTABLISHED	1825
SOURCE	Allt a Mhullin on Ben Nevis
🛢	Remade bourbon hogsheads and fresh ex-sherry butts.
⚗	2
⚗	2

🏚	♿♥▣🛍⛟
☏	01397-700200
	Sept to June, Mon-Fri: 09.00-17.00. July to Aug, Mon-Fri: 09.00-19.30. Sat: 10.00-16.00. Groups by appointment only. Admission charge redeemable in shop.
OTHER ATTRACTIONS	Tearoom.
AWARDS RECEIVED	ASVA commended
VISITORS PER YEAR	30,000

AGE WHEN BOTTLED	26 years
STRENGTH ABV	53.1%

TASTING NOTES

NOSE	Sweet, malty bouquet with rich hints of smoke and vanilla. Very impressive.
TASTE	Envelopes the palate firmly. Rich, full-bodied, aromatic with a delicious length of finish.
COMMENTS	A little water and an oustanding after-dinner dram is to hand. Rare, and bottling strengths will vary according to supply.

BRAND	**Oban**
	✉ Stafford Street, OBAN, Argyll PA34 5NH
	☎ 01631-572000
	🖷 01631-572006
MANAGER	Ian Williams
OWNING COMPANY	UDV
PRODUCTION STATUS	Operational
ESTABLISHED	1794
SOURCE	Loch Gleann a'Bhearraidh
	🛢 Ex-bourbon
	🗚 1
	🗚 1

⑭	🍴♥🖼♿
	☎ 01631-572004
	🖷 01631-572011
	Open all year, Mon-Fri: 09.30-17.00. Easter to Oct: Sat: 09.30-17.00. July to Sept, Mon-Sat: 09.30-20.30. Dec to Feb: by appointment only. Groups by appointment only. Admission charge redeemable in shop.
AWARDS RECEIVED	STB recommended
VISITORS PER YEAR	40,000

AGE WHEN BOTTLED	14 years
STRENGTH ABV	43%
SPECIAL BOTTLINGS	Distiller's Edition, 1980

TASTING NOTES	
NOSE	Fresh hint of peat with a rich but delicate sweetness.
TASTE	Firm, malty flavour finishing with a creamy sweetness.
COMMENTS	A Classic Malt from UDV for drinking at any time.

The Lowlands

HISTORICALLY, the distinguishing features between Highland and Lowland whisky are more numerous than their current-day differences, which can be summarised as stylistic. In the late 18th century the product of the discrete Highland still was a wholesome, hand-crafted spirit which was in great demand in the urban markets. The industrial-scale Lowland distillers, however, produced a coarser whisky (rarely made purely from malted barley alone) in an effort to supply both the city drinkers and the lucrative London market. This situation was created by the Lowland distillers who aggressively exploited whatever Government legislation was in force at the time. The distinctions were further magnified by the creation of the imaginary 'Highland Line', stretching from Greenock on the Clyde to Dundee on the Tay. This created two legislative regions 'gauged' under two separate sets of Excise regulations designed to cope with the disparity between their respective products.

Eventually the technical differences were removed when more realistic early 19th-century Government Acts created a level playing field and encouraged illicit distillers in the Highlands to go legal.

The closures of the big grain distilleries in and around Edinburgh mean that there is little to remind us of the enormous industrial power these concerns once wielded across the central belt of Scotland. Similarly, Lowland malt distilleries were once in abundance even in the late 19th century. In the remote south-west over a dozen concerns existed stretching from Stranraer to Annan. Only Bladnoch Distillery survives and, after a period of closure, will recommence distilling in 1998. The remains of two distilleries at Langholm (Glen Tarras and Langholm) and Annan (Annandale) can still be viewed but they are now merely reminders of a bygone age.

Most of the Lowland malts are now produced to the north along the path of the Highland line. In the Glasgow area, just north of the Clyde along the A82 route to Loch Lomond lies Auchentoshan Distillery, which is the only remaining Lowland distillery still employing the technique of triple-distillation. The other Lowland triple-distilled malt used to be produced at Rosebank, near Falkirk. This is one of the great Lowland malts, highly regarded as a pre-dinner dram and a wonderful surprise to anyone drinking their first malt whisky.

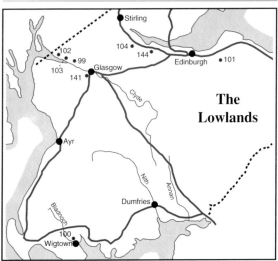

DISTILLERY LOCATION NUMBERS REFER TO PAGE NUMBERS

Although Rosebank was mothballed in 1993 there is a chance that production might recommence on the back of the redevelopment of the Forth & Clyde canal which should be completed in time for the millennium.

To the east of Edinburgh Glenkinchie Distillery at Pencaitland was one of the first to cater for visitors and a brand new facility is now up and running offering one of the most complete visitor experiences of any distillery in Scotland. This stop should be a must for anyone visiting Edinburgh.

Thought For Food

The lack of peatiness, seaweed and coastal brine influence allows Lowland malt to display a softness and malty fruitiness with even a gentle, sweet, lemony feel that matches the more delicate smoked fish dishes and various cheeses. No lovingly prepared picnic hamper should be without a bottle of Lowland malt. Try the combinations listed here.

Glenkinchie 10-year-old and traditional Scottish smoked salmon.

Littlemill 8-year-old with Stichill or Kelsae cheese and oatcakes.

BRAND	**Auchentoshan**
✉	DALMUIR, Dunbartonshire G81 4SG
☏	01389-878561
🖷	01389-877368
MANAGER	Stuart Hodkinson
OWNING COMPANY	Morrison Bowmore Distillers Ltd
PRODUCTION STATUS	Operational
ESTABLISHED	1823
SOURCE	Kilpatrick Hills
🛢	Ex-bourbon and sherry
🍶	1
🍶	1
AWARDS RECEIVED	1992/94 IWSC: Gold Medal: 21-y.o.

AGE WHEN BOTTLED	No age given (Select), 10 & 21 years
STRENGTH ABV	Select & 10-y.o: 40%; 21-y.o: 43%
SPECIAL BOTTLINGS	22 & 25-y.o Ceramics @ 43%

TASTING NOTES

NOSE	Delicate, slightly sweet and floral.
TASTE	Light, soft and sweet with a slightly fruity aftertaste.
COMMENTS	Triple-distilled in the traditional Lowland style and widely available.

BRAND	**Bladnoch**
✉	BLADNOCH, Wigtownshire DG8 9AB
☎	01988-402235
🖷	01988-402605
MANAGER	Raymond Armstrong
OWNING COMPANY	Co-ordinated Development Services Ltd
PRODUCTION STATUS	Seasonally operational
ESTABLISHED	1817
SOURCE	River Bladnoch
🛢	Ex-bourbon and sherry
🍶	1
🍶	1

(icons)	
☎	01988-402605
	Easter to Oct, Mon-Fri: 10.00-16.00. Nov to Dec, 11.00-15.30.
OTHER ATTRACTIONS	Woodland and river walks, picnic areas, fishing, canoeing, camping, art events. Wigtown is Scotland's Booktown.
VISITORS PER YEAR	20,000

AGE WHEN BOTTLED	10 years
STRENGTH ABV	43%

TASTING NOTES	
NOSE	Very light, aromatic, delicate and fruity.
TASTE	Smooth, delicate and sweet but full and stimulating. Moreish.
COMMENTS	Distilling will recommence in 1998 on a limited basis. A welcome return.

BRAND	**Glenkinchie**
	✉ PENCAITLAND, East Lothian EH34 5ET
	☎ 01875-342003
	📠 01875-342001
MANAGER	Brian Bisset
OWNING COMPANY	UDV
PRODUCTION STATUS	Operational
ESTABLISHED	1837
SOURCE	Lammermuir Hills
	🛢 Ex-bourbon
	🥃 1
	🥃 1

(visitor info)

☎ 01875-342002
📠 01875-342007

A brilliant facility. Make sure you visit this if you are in Edinburgh. Open all year, Mon-Fri: 09.30-17.00. May to Sept, Sat: 09.00-16.00. Sun: 12.00-16.00. Groups by appointment only. Admission charge redeemable in shop.

VISITORS PER YEAR	20,000

AGE WHEN BOTTLED	10 years
STRENGTH ABV	43%
SPECIAL BOTTLINGS	Distiller's Edition, 1986

TASTING NOTES	
NOSE	Light, fragrant, sweetness with a trace of peat.
TASTE	Round flavour, slightly dry with a lingering smoothness. Well-balanced.
COMMENTS	Pre-dinner Classic Malt from UDV.

MALT	**Inverleven**
✉	DUMBARTON, Dunbartonshire G82 1ND
☎	01389-765111
🖷	01389-723081
OWNING COMPANY	Allied Distillers Ltd
PRODUCTION STATUS	Mothballed 1991
ESTABLISHED	1938
SOURCE	Loch Lomond
🛢	Ex-bourbon
🍶	1
🍶	1

TASTING NOTES	17-year-old, 46%
NOSE	Delicate hint of smoke. A hint of dryness.
TASTE	Quite full-bodied. Smooth with a round palate and a background nuance of fruit.
COMMENTS	Rarely available unless obtained from one of the independent bottlers. See pages 153-154.

BRAND	**Littlemill**
✉	BOWLING, Dunbartonshire G60 5BG
☎	01389-874154
MANAGER	J. Peterson
OWNING COMPANY	Loch Lomond Distillery Co Ltd
PRODUCTION STATUS	Mothballed 1992
ESTABLISHED	1772
SOURCE	Kilpatrick Hills
🛢	Ex-bourbon
⚗	1
⚗	1

AGE WHEN BOTTLED	8 years
STRENGTH ABV	40%
EXPORT BOTTLINGS	40 & 43%

TASTING NOTES

NOSE	Light and delicate, dry and fruity.
TASTE	Mellow-flavoured, light, slightly cloying, yet pleasant and warming.
COMMENTS	Pre-dinner, from a distillery full of interesting, novel features. Certainly one of the oldest in Scotland but it may be gone for good soon.

BRAND	**Rosebank**
✉	Camelon, FALKIRK, Stirlingshire FK1 5BW
☎	01324-623325
OWNING COMPANY	UDV
PRODUCTION STATUS	Mothballed 1993
ESTABLISHED	c1840
SOURCE	Carron Valley reservoir
🛢	Ex-bourbon
🍾	1
🍾	2

AGE WHEN BOTTLED	12 years
STRENGTH ABV	43%
SPECIAL BOTTLINGS	1981 @ 63.9%

TASTING NOTES

NOSE	Light, delicate hints of apple sweetness.
TASTE	Well-balanced, good flavour with a touch of citrus and acceptable astringency.
COMMENTS	A triple-distilled malt suitable for pre-dinner drinking. The resurgence of the Forth & Clyde Canal may help to save this famous malt.

Islay

ISLAY malt whisky is perhaps the most characteristic of all. However, the island's product – traditionally the heaviest and most pungent available – does conceal a few surprises. The most recognisable characteristics are due to production methods which were developed in concert with the available distilling ingredients in this remote locality. While the urban markets were supplied by mainland distillers in the 18th and 19th centuries, the islanders supplied local markets from stills – both legal and illegal – which were operated from farmyards, bothies on the bleak moors above Port Ellen and remote caves along the precipitous coast of the Oa.

Islay, renowned as the most fertile island in the Hebrides, had three major assets in this development: a ready source of local bere or barley, inexhaustible amounts of peat and burns running brim-full of soft water. Coupled to this was the likelihood that the art of distilling was probably brought to Scotland via Islay from Ireland in the 15th century. It is impossible to visit Islay and not notice the peat. Crossing the enormous Laggan Moss between Port Ellen and Bowmore, the peat banks spread as far as the eye can see. This fuel was the only means by which the islanders could dry their grain – an essential process not only for distilling, but also for storage during the wet seasons. By kilning barley it could be kept longer and the dryer the grain was, the less likely it was to go mouldy.

As the grain dried in the fumes, the peat imparted to the barley a highly distinctive character which manifested itself when the spirit was finally distilled from it. These characteristics are still apparent in today's Islay malts and are best experienced by trying Ardbeg, Lagavulin and Laphroaig which form the three most traditional Islay malts. The other Islays display this peaty-smoky characteristic to a lesser degree but it is always detectable nonetheless.

It is good to see that the Islay distillers, despite their more remote location, are always able to accommodate visitors and some of the distilleries are spectacularly situated. All of them have one thing in common – they are built on the seashore. A century and a half ago this afforded them access to the sea and thus the mainland markets. The smaller inland farmyard distilleries were by then falling victim to their more remote locations and closing down. But it is

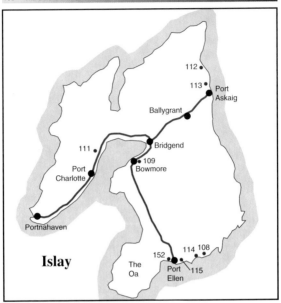

DISTILLERY LOCATION NUMBERS REFER TO PAGE NUMBERS

still possible to view some of these sites at Octomore Farm behind Port Charlotte, Tallant Farm above Bowmore and Lossit Kennels by Bridgend. Of the present distilleries perhaps Bowmore is most favourably endowed for the visitor although Laphroag, Lagavulin and most recently Ardbeg are all catering for visitors well.

On a more sobering note Port Ellen Distillery will never reopen and although Bruichladdich is distilling on an occasional basis, its future is far from secure. The associated maltings behind Port Ellen are, at least, supplying not only Lagavulin and Caol Ila with malt, but also some of the other non-UDV distilleries on the island.

Bruichladdich which, like Bunnahabhain, produces one of the lighter Islays was one of the first in the Hebrides to be constructed from concrete in 1881. Near Port Askaig, at the point where you take the ferry crossing to Jura, lie Caol Ila and Bunnahabhain with spectacular views of the Paps of Jura. Caol Ila is as modern and efficient a distillery as you are likely to find and the stillhouse alone is worth seeing. The dram is a good Islay, as is its close neighbour which was built in 1880-1.

Bunnahabhain is for many people the best introduction to the Islays since it is neither too heavy nor too light, and for many it remains their favourite Islay dram. The Islays should be approached with great respect since they are considered as essential components by master-blenders who, without them, would be left with a very much reduced palette from which to create the Scotch blends which have been the bedrock of the industry's success the world over.

Thought For Food

Quite simply these whiskies are so flavoursome on their own that there are few foods that can stand up to them. Speciality continental sausages can work along with certain blue cheeses and fresh nuts. Try my combination below instead of port and cheese.

Bowmore 10-year-old with Lanark Blue cheese, hazelnuts and oatcakes.

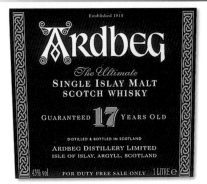

BRAND	**Ardbeg**
	✉ PORT ELLEN, Islay, Argyll PA42 7DU
	☎ 01496-302244
	📠 01496-302040
MANAGER	Stuart Thomson
OWNING COMPANY	Glenmorangie plc
PRODUCTION STATUS	Operational
ESTABLISHED	1815
SOURCE	Lochs Uigeadale and Iarnam
🛢	American oak barrels
🍾	1
🍾	1

(🏛)

🏕🖥♿

Open all year. Mon-Fri: 10.00-16.00. Jun-Aug, Sat: 10.00-16.00. £2 admission charge redeemable in shop.

OTHER ATTRACTIONS	The Old Kiln Coffee Shop

AGE WHEN BOTTLED	1978 & 17 years
STRENGTH ABV	1978: 43%, 17-y.o: 40%
SPECIAL BOTTLINGS	30-y.o @ 43%; Provenance, 1974 @ 55.6%

TASTING NOTES	17-year-old
NOSE	Lovely full aroma with peat-sweet overtones.
TASTE	Full-bodied and luscious with an intense Islay flavour and excellent aftertaste.
COMMENTS	A stunning after-dinner malt. Now reissued and sure to do well. Beginners beware! Expect to pay around £250 for a bottle of Provenance.

BRAND	**Bowmore**
	(Beau-more)
✉	BOWMORE, Islay, Argyll PA43 7JS
☎	01496-810441
🖷	01496-810757
MANAGER	Islay Campbell
OWNING COMPANY	Morrison Bowmore Distillers Ltd
PRODUCTION STATUS	Operational
ESTABLISHED	1779
SOURCE	River Laggan
🛢	Ex-bourbon and sherry
⌂	Floor maltings
🍶	2
🍶	2

	🚻 ♿ 🛍
☎	01496-810441
	Open all year. Mon-Fri: tours at 10.30 & 14.00. May to Oct: 11.30 & 15.00. Sat: 10.30. Groups by appointment only. £2 admission charge redeemable in shop.
AWARDS RECEIVED	1996 IWSC: Best Single Malt up to 12 years old: Legend.
VISITORS PER YEAR	10,000

AGE WHEN BOTTLED	No age given (Legend, Darkest), 12, 15 (Mariner), 17 & 21 years
STRENGTH ABV	Legend & 12-y.o: 40%; all others: 43%
SPECIAL BOTTLINGS	Cask Strength @ 56%; 25 & 30-y.o Ceramics @ 43%
EXPORT BOTTLINGS	Legend, 12, 17, 21, 22, 25 & 30-y.o., Black.

TASTING NOTES   12-year-old

NOSE   Light, peaty-smoky with a bewitching aroma of honey-
                     suckle.

TASTE   Medium-bodied, succulent, slightly peaty with a good
                     aftertaste.

COMMENTS   A fine Islay in a plethora of bottlings. Something for
                     everyone. The swimming pool at the entrance to the
                     distillery is heated by the plant's waste heat!

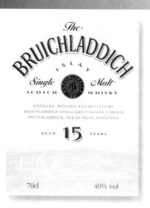

70cl   40% vol

BRAND	**Bruichladdich**
	(Broo-ich-laddie)
✉	BRUICHLADDICH, Islay, Argyll PA49 7UN
☎	01496-850221
MANAGER	Willie Tait
OWNING COMPANY	Jim Beam Brands (Greater Europe) plc
PRODUCTION STATUS	Intermittently operational
ESTABLISHED	1881
SOURCE	Private dam
⚗	2
⚗	2

AGE WHEN BOTTLED	10, 15 & 21 years
STRENGTH ABV	40%
SPECIAL BOTTLINGS	Stillman's Dram, currently 26 years
EXPORT BOTTLINGS	10, 15 & 21 y.o., 40 & 43%

TASTING NOTES	10-year-old
NOSE	Light to medium with a good hint of smoke. Slightly dry.
TASTE	Lingering flavour giving the expected fullness of Islay character whilst lacking the heavier tones.
COMMENTS	A good pre-dinner dram, which is an ideal introduction to the Islay style. The 15-year-old is superb.

BRAND	**Bunnahabhain**
	(Bunna-ha-venn)
✉	PORT ASKAIG, Islay, Argyll PA46 7RP
☎	01496-840646
🖷	01496-840248
MANAGER	Hamish Proctor
OWNING COMPANY	Highland Distillers
PRODUCTION STATUS	Operational
ESTABLISHED	1881
SOURCE	Margadale Springs
🛢	Ex-bourbon
⚗	2
⚗	2

⑭	⚙🖵
	Open all year. Mon-Fri: 10.00-16.00. By appointment only.
VISITORS PER YEAR	1,000

AGE WHEN BOTTLED	12 years
STRENGTH ABV	40%
EXPORT BOTTLINGS	43%

TASTING NOTES	
NOSE	Pronounced yet delicately sweet character with a flowery aroma.
TASTE	Not reminiscent of the Islay style, but a lovely round, medium-sweet flavour nonetheless. Finishes with a subdued smokiness.
COMMENTS	A popular after-dinner dram especially in France and the United States.

BRAND	**Caol Ila**
	(Cull-eela)
✉	PORT ASKAIG, Islay, Argyll PA46 7RL
☎	01496-840207
🖷	01496-840660
MANAGER	Mike Nicolson
OWNING COMPANY	UDV
PRODUCTION STATUS	Operational
ESTABLISHED	1846
SOURCE	Loch Nam Ban
🛢	Ex-bourbon and sherry
🍶	3
🍶	3

🏠 ♿▣

Open all year. Mon-Fri, by appointment only. Admission charge redeemable in shop.

OTHER ATTRACTIONS	The views from the stillhouse over to Jura!
VISITORS PER YEAR	2,000

AGE WHEN BOTTLED	15 years
STRENGTH ABV	43%
SPECIAL BOTTLINGS	21-y.o @ 61.3% Rare Malts Selection; 1981 @ 63.8%

TASTING NOTES	15-year-old
NOSE	Light, fresh, slightly peated but unmistakably Islay.
TASTE	Medium-bodied with a dry, rounded flavour. Finishes smoothly. Not as heavy as some other Islays but carries an agreeable degree of pungency.
COMMENTS	Popular after-dinner dram. Sherried bottlings are excellent.

BRAND	**Lagavulin**
	(Lagga-voolin)
✉	PORT ELLEN, Islay, Argyll PA42 7DZ
☎	01496-302400/250
🖷	01496-302321
MANAGER	Mike Nicolson
OWNING COMPANY	UDV
PRODUCTION STATUS	Operational
ESTABLISHED	1816 with distilling on site since 1784 at least.
SOURCE	Solum Lochs
🛢	Ex-bourbon and sherry
♂	2
♂	2

☎	01496-302217
	Open all year. Mon-Fri, by appointment only. Admission charge redeemable in shop.
OTHER ATTRACTIONS	The ruins of the Macdonald stronghold of Dun Naomhaig (Dunn-aaveg) stand nearby.
VISITORS PER YEAR	3,000

AGE WHEN BOTTLED	16 years
STRENGTH ABV	43%
SPECIAL BOTTLINGS	Distiller's Edition, 1979

TASTING NOTES	
NOSE	Heavy, powerful, peat-smoke aroma. Unmistakably Islay with a big, sherry character.
TASTE	Robustly full-bodied, well-balanced and smooth with a hint of sherry sweetness on the palate. Lingering finish.
COMMENTS	One of United Distillers' Classic Malt range. A remarkable Islay malt and a great way to round off a hearty meal.

BRAND	**Laphroaig**
	(La-froyg)
✉	PORT ELLEN, Islay, Argyll PA42 7DU
☎	01496-302418
📠	01496-302496
MANAGER	Iain Henderson
OWNING COMPANY	Allied Distillers Ltd
PRODUCTION STATUS	Operational
ESTABLISHED	1815
SOURCE	Kilbride Dam
🛢	Ex-Kentucky bourbon
⌂	Floor maltings
🍶	3
🍶	4

	♿
	Sept to June, Mon-Thu: tours at 10.30 & 14.30. Fri: 10.30. By appointment only.
OTHER ATTRACTIONS	Write to the distillery to become a 'Friend of Laphroaig'.
AWARDS RECEIVED	1997 IWSC: Most Outstanding Malt, Cask Strength
VISITORS PER YEAR	5,000

AGE WHEN BOTTLED	10, 15 years
STRENGTH ABV	10-y.o: 40%; 15-y.o: 43%
SPECIAL BOTTLINGS	Duty free: 1977 @ 43%; 10-y.o Cask Strength @ 57.3%
EXPORT BOTTLINGS	43% for export.

TASTING NOTES	10-year-old
NOSE	Unmistakable. Medicinal, well-balanced, peaty-smoky. Delightfully pungent.
TASTE	Full of character, big peaty flavour with a delightful touch of lingering sweetness. Betrays its proximity to sea.
COMMENTS	An excellent after-dinner malt from a beautifully situated distillery. Very popular.

Campbeltown

SITUATED on the lee shore of the Mull of Kintyre, this town was literally awash with distillate just over a hundred years ago. When Alfred Barnard compiled his wonderful book *The Whisky Distilleries of the United Kingdom* in 1886, he found no less than 21 producing distilleries in and around the town.

These were Hazelburn (established 1836), Springbank (1828), Dalintober (1832), Benmore (1868), Ardlussa (1879), Dalaruan (1824), Lochead (1824), Glen Nevis (1877), Kinloch (1823), Burnside (1825), Glengyle (1873), Lochruan (1835), Albyn (1830), Scotia (1832), Rieclachan (1825), Glenside (1830), Longrow (1824), Kintyre (c1826), Campbeltown(1815), Argyll (1844) and Springside (1830).

These operations were a throwback to the days when illicit distillation in the district around the town was rife, and this was not entirely discouraged by the landowners or indeed by the law. Campbeltown's boom period was based upon a ready and huge market in cheap Scotch within the working population in the industrial central belt and the avaricious desire of the distillers to supply that market, come what may.

A local coal seam was a convenient source of cheap fuel, but its exhaustion was to prove fatal, and as the late Victorian boom in whisky distilling collapsed so too did distilling in Campbeltown. The remnants of that period are to be found in the numerous street names and old distillery buildings which can still be found in the town, but only two distilleries actually remain: Glen Scotia and Springbank, of which only Springbank is currently producing two styles of whisky.

It would be unwise to forget Campbeltown's contribution to distilling despite the fact that it is unlikely more distilleries will ever start up in the town again. Its whisky had a unique regional flavour which came close to the Islay style which can still be found in Longrow, a traditional old-fashioned malt which is distilled at Springbank. Its character differs from its sister malt Springbank which is a smoother, more elegant dram. A recent development has been the distillation of a unique millennium dram at Springbank which involves the use of only organic barley, grown completely free of outside interference from pesticides or chemical fertilisers. I await the outcome of this innovation with interest.

Barnard's visit coincided with the 'Golden Age' of distilling in Scotland – a time we are unlikely to experience again. If Campbeltown's decline has served any purpose at all, it will have been to remind us all of the fickle nature of the marketplace and the awful consequences of boom and bust economics.

As a town, Campbeltown is delightfully situated. Its remoteness allows its inhabitants a certain privacy from the mainstream tourist traffic during the summer, but it is always worth considering the detour down the Mull of Kintyre when travelling through Argyll. The recent establishment of a ferry service to and from Ballycastle in Northern Ireland is bound to help increase the number of visitors and I hope that the town's malts might even find themselves with a following in Co Antrim, home of their close neighbour, Bushmills!

Thought For Food

The distinctive malts of Campbeltown are well-suited to some blue cheeses and smoked fish.

Springbank 15-year-old with fillet of halibut, coated in honey and smoked over beech wood and juniper.

BRAND	**Glen Scotia**
✉	12 High Street, CAMPBELTOWN, Argyll PA28 6DS
☎	01586-552288
MANAGER	J. Peterson
OWNING COMPANY	Loch Lomond Distillery Co Ltd
PRODUCTION STATUS	Mothballed 1994
ESTABLISHED	1832
SOURCE	Campbeltown Loch
🛢	Ex-bourbon
🍾	1
🥃	1

AGE WHEN BOTTLED	14 years
STRENGTH ABV	40%
EXPORT BOTTLINGS	43%

TASTING NOTES

NOSE	An intense aroma with a touch of smoke. Delicate and sweet.
TASTE	Light for a Campbeltown with a hint of peat and a delicate, sweet, clean finish of medium length.
COMMENTS	A pre-dinner dram. In fact, a good drink at any time.

BRAND	**Longrow**
DISTILLERY	Springbank
✉	CAMPBELTOWN, Argyll PA28 6ET
☎	01586-552085
🖷	01586-553215
MANAGER	Frank McHardy
OWNING COMPANY	J & A Mitchell & Co Ltd
PRODUCTION STATUS	Operational
ESTABLISHED	1828
SOURCE	Crosshill Loch
🛢	Refill whisky, ex-sherry and bourbon
🏠	Floor maltings
🍸	1
🍷	2
OTHER ATTRACTIONS	The bottling hall.

AGE WHEN BOTTLED	10 years
STRENGTH ABV	46%

TASTING NOTES

NOSE	A light, island-peaty, medicinal aroma with sweet overtones.
TASTE	Well-balanced, with a hint of sweetness and smoke. A succulent malty palate and a fine lingering aftertaste.
COMMENTS	Distilled at Springbank, but by using entirely peat-dried malted barley, the heavier peated malt results. A dram for the connoisseur, a 1973 cask of which was recently available.

BRAND	**Springbank**
✉	CAMPBELTOWN, Argyll PA28 6ET
☎	01586-552085
🖷	01586-553215
MANAGER	Frank McHardy
OWNING COMPANY	J & A Mitchell & Co Ltd
PRODUCTION STATUS	Operational
ESTABLISHED	1828
SOURCE	Crosshill Loch
🛢	Refill whisky, ex-sherry and bourbon
⌂	Floor maltings
♨	1
♨	2
OTHER ATTRACTIONS	The bottling hall.

AGE WHEN BOTTLED	12 & 21years
STRENGTH ABV	46%
SPECIAL BOTTLINGS	1966, local barley distillation @ cask strength; Chairman's Vat @ 46%

TASTING NOTES	21-year-old
NOSE	Positive, rich aroma with a slight yet assertive sweetness.
TASTE	Well-balanced, charming and elegant. Rich and full of deep flavour. A malt drinker's dream.
COMMENTS	A dependable classic for the malt lover and a superb after-dinner drink. Bottled at the distillery and widely available.

The Islands

ARCHAEOLOGICAL discoveries on the island of Rhum in the Inner Hebrides suggest that the natives knew how to make a brew long before the Irish were credited with introducing the art of distillation to their Scottish cousins. William Grant & Sons Ltd (makers of Balvenie, Kininvie and Glenfiddich and owners of Convalmore) even went so far as to try and recreate the original 4000-year-old recipe which was scientifically reconstructed from scrapings off pottery shards. This brew was drawn from the local herbs, grasses and other vegetation and turned out to be a little immature, but like all good brews it improved with familiarity.

The last two centuries may have gradually familiarised the world to Scotch, but we can now lay claim to having played a fundamental part in the history of the development of distillation. And for the present-day visitor to Scotland, the past is manifested in some of the most gloriously situated distilleries in the world.

The most recent addition to the island portfolio is the distillery at Lochranza which, as we go to press, will be legally entitled to call its three-year-old spirit Scotch malt whisky. My reflections on the two-year-old are on page 124 and my feelings are that this malt will be outstanding in years to come. Visitor facilities at the distillery are very good and the location is breathtaking.

The styles of the other island malts differ, partly due to location and partly due to the desires of the distillery operators. For instance Jura, from the island just north of Islay, can be fairly described as a Highland-like dram whereas in the last century it was much closer in style to its Islay neighbours. The reason is that the distillery went out of production in 1901 and was replaced in 1963 with a completely new unit designed by the Welsh distillery builder William Delmé-Evans. He had stills of a highland-type design installed and used malt that was only lightly peated. Similarly Tobermory's distillery has had its plant changed over the years and has produced some variable distillations of Ledaig until ceasing production in 1980. Happily, it came back on stream in May 1990 and is now under the ownership of Burn Stewart.

On Skye an altogether more traditional taste is found. Talisker is one of the giants among malt. It is a 'big' whisky in every way with an explosive effect

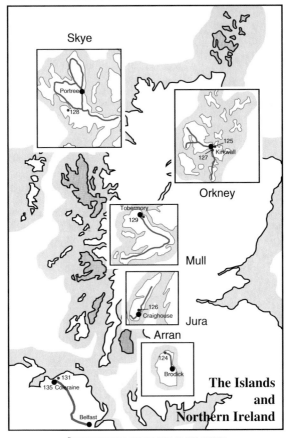

DISTILLERY LOCATION NUMBERS REFER TO PAGE NUMBERS

on the palate and a wonderful, peaty, sweetness on the nose. The distillery has changed considerably but still retains some of the more traditional implements associated with 18th and 19th-century distilling. For instance, swan-necked lyne arms can be seen dropping into wooden worm tubs outside the stillhouse wall – the same technique illicit distillers used in their bothies. Notwithstanding the untested Arran distillate, Talisker's taste is perhaps the most recognisable among the island and western malts and has benefitted greatly from being included in the Classic Malts selection from UDV.

Orkney is the most northerly outpost of whisky distilling in Scotland with two very good malts emanating from Highland Park and Scapa. Sadly the latter is still lying dormant but a new bottling by owners Allied Distillers has made a welcome return. Highland Park is currently bottling some outstanding vintages that are creating great interest.

With Lochranza now on stream and Tobermory back in the production, island distilling seems to be on the upswing as we enter the new millennium. Something worth drinking (and eating) to!

Thought For Food

Jura

Isle of Jura 10-year-old with mature cheddar and oatcakes.

This whisky is suited to many cheddar-style cheeses, the stronger the better. Try it with fresh walnuts as an added treat.

Mull

Tobermory and smoked mussels.

The malt's aromatic sweetness and gentle smokiness on the finish is just the right balance for this seafood accompaniment.

Skye

Talisker 10-year-old and Stornoway black pudding served with a coarse apple and raspberry sauce.

The explosive flavours of these island products along with the calming and refreshing fruitiness of the sauce is an unique combination.

Orkney

Highland Park 12-year-old with smoked Orkney cheese and Stockan's oatcakes.

It simply has to be. If you can get the traditional cheese matured in a barrel of oatmeal it is an added bonus. The finishing subtle dryness of the malt and smoky creaminess of this cheese is perfection.

BRAND	**Isle of Arran**
DISTILLERY	Lochranza
✉	Isle of Arran, Argyll KA27 8HJ
☎	01770-830334
🖷	01770-830611
MANAGER	Gordon Mitchell
OWNING COMPANY	Isle of Arran Distillers Ltd
PRODUCTION STATUS	Operational
ESTABLISHED	1995
SOURCE	Eason Biorach (Mountain Burn)
🛢	Ex-sherry hogsheads, butts and puncheons
♨	1
♨	1

(★)	♨🎥📺♿
☎	01770-830264
🖷	01770-830364
	Mon-Sun: 10.00-18.00, last tour at 17.00. During winter, telephone in advance to confirm whether reception centre is open. Coach parties welcome, but should telephone in advance. Contact: Marion Noble.
OTHER ATTRACTIONS	Guided tours, restaurant open for lunch and dinner.
VISITORS PER YEAR	40,000

AGE WHEN BOTTLED	New spirit, 2 years old, distilled June 1995
STRENGTH ABV	60%

TASTING NOTES	
NOSE	Big, round malty aroma with delicate, sweet overtones.
TASTE	Malt and sweetness come through as expected in a new spirit.
COMMENTS	This new island dram will have a considerable future after it comes of age in June 1998.

BRAND	**Highland Park**
	✉ KIRKWALL, Orkney KW15 1SU
	☎ 01856-873107
	🖷 01856-876091
MANAGER	James Robertson
OWNING COMPANY	Highland Distillers
PRODUCTION STATUS	Operational
ESTABLISHED	1798
SOURCE	Cattie Maggie's Spring
	🛢 Ex-bourbon and sherry
	⛲ Floor maltings
	🍶 2
	🍶 2

🏭 ・ 🎁 🎞 📺 ♿

☎ 01856-874619

🖷 01856-876091

Apr to Oct, Mon-Fri: 10.00-17.00, last tour at 16.00. July to Aug, Sat-Sun: 12.00-17.00. Nov to Mar, Mon-Fri: tour at 14.00. Closed between Xmas and New Year. Groups by appointment only. Admission charge redeemable in shop.

VISITORS PER YEAR	18,000

AGE WHEN BOTTLED	12, 18 & 25 years
STRENGTH ABV	12-y.o: 40%; 18-y.o: 43%; 25-y.o: 54%
EXPORT BOTTLINGS	43%

TASTING NOTES	12-year-old
NOSE	Full of character – pleasant, lingering against a smoky, delicate background.
TASTE	Medium-bodied, well-balanced with good length. Finishes with a subtle, smoky dryness.
COMMENTS	An excellent after-dinner dram. The 18 year old is terrific.

BRAND	**Isle of Jura**
✉	CRAIGHOUSE, Isle of Jura, Argyll PA60 7XT
☎	01496-820240
🖷	01496-820344
MANAGER	Willie Tait
OWNING COMPANY	Jim Beam Brands (Greater Europe) plc
PRODUCTION STATUS	Operational
ESTABLISHED	c1810, rebuilt 1960-63
SOURCE	Loch A'Bhaile Mhargaidh (or Market Loch)
🛢	American white oak, small proportion of oloroso sherry butts
🍶	2
🍶	2

(IM)

Sept to May, Mon-Fri: 09.00-16.00, by appointment only.

AGE WHEN BOTTLED	10 years
STRENGTH ABV	40%
SPECIAL BOTTLINGS	Stillman's Dram, currently 26 years
EXPORT BOTTLINGS	43%

TASTING NOTES	10-year-old
NOSE	Dry and tart. Smooth with subtle peaty traces.
TASTE	Well-matured, full but delicate floral aspects. Good, round, lingering character.
COMMENTS	An almost Highland-like malt created by W. Delmé-Evans.

BRAND	**Scapa**
	✉ KIRKWALL, Orkney KW15 1SE
	☎ 01856-872071
	🖷 01856-876585
MANAGER	Ronnie MacDonald
OWNING COMPANY	Allied Distillers Ltd
PRODUCTION STATUS	Mothballed 1994
ESTABLISHED	1824
SOURCE	Lingro Burn and local springs
	🛢 Ex-bourbon barrels
	🍶 1
	🍶 1

🏭

Tours by arrangement.

AGE WHEN BOTTLED	12 years
STRENGTH ABV	40%

TASTING NOTES	1985, 40%
NOSE	Delightful aromatic bouquet of peat and heather. Slightly rich.
TASTE	Medium-bodied with a malty, sweet, silk-like finish. Good, firm, long-lasting flavour.
COMMENTS	After-dinner.

BRAND	**Talisker**
✉	CARBOST, Isle of Skye, IV47 8SR
☎	01478-640203
🖷	01478-640401
MANAGER	Mike Copland
OWNING COMPANY	UDV
PRODUCTION STATUS	Operational
ESTABLISHED	1830
SOURCE	Cnoc-nan-Speireag (hawkhill)
🛢	Ex-bourbon and sherry
🍶	2
🍶	3

(H)	♨ ♥ 🖵 ᵫ
☎	01478-640314
🖷	01478-640401
	Apr to Oct, Mon-Fri: 09.00-16.30. July to Aug, Mon-Sat: 09.30-16.30. Nov to Mar, Mon-Fri: 14.00-16.30. Dec to Feb, by appointment only. Admission charge redeemable in shop. Groups by appointment only. No coaches.
AWARDS RECEIVED	1997 IWSC: Gold Medal. 1997 International Spirits Challenge: Best Single Malt under 12 years.
VISITORS PER YEAR	42,000

AGE WHEN BOTTLED	10 years
STRENGTH ABV	45.8%
SPECIAL BOTTLINGS	Distiller's Edition, 1986

TASTING NOTES	
NOSE	Heavy, sweet and full aroma with gentle smoky overtones.
TASTE	Unique full-bodied flavour of peaches and cream which explodes on the palate, lingering sweetly then fading to light smoke.
COMMENTS	Superb after-dinner malt from UDV's Classic Malts.

BRAND	**Tobermory**
✉	TOBERMORY, Isle of Mull, Argyll PA75 6NR
☎	01688-302645
📠	01688-302643
MANAGER	Ian Macmillan. Asst: Alan McConnochie
OWNING COMPANY	Burn Stewart Distillers plc
PRODUCTION STATUS	Operational
ESTABLISHED	1798
SOURCE	Private loch
🛢	American and Spanish oak hogsheads and butts
♠	2
♠	2

⑭	🎬🍸🖼♿
☎	01688-302647
📠	01688-302643
	Easter to Oct, Mon-Fri: 10.00-17.00. Oct to Easter, by appointment only. Groups by appointment only. Admission charge redeemable in shop.
VISITORS PER YEAR	8,000

AGE WHEN BOTTLED	No age given
STRENGTH ABV	40%

TASTING NOTES

NOSE	A light but definite sweetness with soft, gentle overtones of fruit.
TASTE	Good, light to medium flavour, softly aromatic, sweet overtones which give good balance. Finishes with a hint of smokiness.
COMMENTS	A most welcome island malt made from unpeated barley. Also available as Ledaig, 1974 at 43%, made from peated barley. See pages 153-154.

Northern Ireland

TODAY whiskey-making in the province is solely represented by Bushmills in County Antrim, but it was once much more widespread with distilleries such as Avoniel, Connswater, Royal Irish (all Co Antrim), Comber in Co Down, and Abbey Street, Waterside, Coleraine and Limavady in Co Londonderry.

Irish whiskey is distilled from a mash containing both malted and unmalted barley, but the main difference between Scotch malt and the Irish variety is that the latter is distilled three times as opposed to twice. This means that many of the characteristic elements which are retained during double distillation are removed when the spirit is triple distilled. In general the result is a whiskey of lighter character.

Old Bushmills Distillery caters well for the whiskey enthusiast and is situated on the stunning Co Antrim coastline overlooking the North Channel to Scotland, which might well be the very stretch of water over which the secrets of distilling were taken many hundreds of years ago. Such a heritage is perhaps more apparent from the fact that the distillery received its first licence to distil on 20 April, 1608 with a tradition of activity on the site stretching even further back to 1276. Bushmills has produced some special bottlings lately and will be ensuring that the millennium does not go unheeded! Notwithstanding the discoveries on Rhum, there can be little doubt that the Scots owe their distilling pedigree to a large degree to their Irish cousins.

Thought For Food

Bushmills 10-year-old malt whiskey

This whiskey's combination of flavours are so versatile that it is equally delicious when paired with dishes such as smoked oysters or with the distillery's own Bushmill's-soaked fruit cake.

BRAND	**Bushmills**
	BUSHMILLS, Co. Antrim, BT57 8XH
	01265-731521
	01265-731339
MANAGER	Dave Quinn
OWNING COMPANY	Irish Distillers Group Ltd
PRODUCTION STATUS	Operational
ESTABLISHED	1608
SOURCE	St Columb's Rill
	Ex-bourbon and sherry, some port pipes
	4
	5

	01265-731521
	01265-731339
	Nov to Mar, Mon-Fri, tours at 10.00, 11.00, 12.00, 13.30, 14.30, 15.30. Apr to Oct, Mon-Sat: tours between 09.30 and 16.30. Sun: 12.00-16.00. Closed Good Friday after 12.00.
OTHER ATTRACTIONS	Giant's Causeway and Dunluce Castle are nearby.
AWARDS RECEIVED	1995 IWSC: Gold Medal
VISITORS PER YEAR	100,000

AGE WHEN BOTTLED	10 years
STRENGTH ABV	40%
SPECIAL BOTTLINGS	12-y.o Distillery Reserve. 16-y.o 'Three Woods'. Duty free: 10-y.o @ 43%
EXPORT BOTTLINGS	5-y.o in Italy. 10-y.o @43%

TASTING NOTES	10-year-old
NOSE	Warm, slightly smoky, sweet bouquet with hints of sherry, vanilla and honey.
TASTE	Smooth and malty. Well-rounded, mellow with a fine combination of flavours.
COMMENTS	Triple-distilled for mellowness and an increasingly popular malt from the world's oldest licensed distillery.

Lost Distilleries

THE following distilleries are non-operational due to the fact that they are either no longer in existence, or closed and have no prospect of reopening. Their product is still available from various sources and labels from the independent bottlers have been reproduced along with some of the Rare Malts Selection available from UDV.

The first group – defunct distilleries – do not exist any more. In some cases a vestige of the original structure remains (such as St Magdalene at Linlithgow), but these malts really have gone forever. The second group – closed distilleries – still exist, but are essentially ghost structures which may eventually find alternative uses. In almost every case, they are unlikely to open again.

The reasons for these closures are almost always the same. The whisky industry has, over the last 100 years, been subject to a cyclical pattern of supply and demand. In many cases distilleries were owned by companies which found that they had too much bonded stock on hand at times when supply far outstripped demand. In these circumstances many distilleries were shut down in order to conserve stocks and reduce production capacity and overheads. The more remote the distillery, the more likely it was to be closed. Furthermore, those distilleries which lacked the cachet of some of the more prominent 'crack' whiskies and which produced malt solely for the fillings trade, were also vulnerable.

Many of these distilleries also suffered from compromised design and lack of convenient access for modern transport. Furthermore, distillery closures often occur when companies merge and the whisky industry has been no stranger to this as witness the recent mega-merger to create Diageo. These developments have almost always served to reduce the whisky heritage throughout Scotland. As I reported in the last edition, Lochside Distillery in Montrose was closed but not then considered lost. Regrettably, the situation has changed and the distillery, whilst still standing, has been cleared of plant and awaits the demolition men. Only the law can stop them. A friend who recently returned from Mallorca managed to snap up a few of the remaining bottles of Lochside at the ridiculous price of 1100 Pesetas a bottle (less than £4.50, duty paid!). This shrewd deal was due to the fact that the Spanish owners had made the malt more available abroad than at home.

But this selection is all about nostalgia and the chance to snap up a little of Scotland's history before it is lost forever. Almost all of these whiskies are available from the specialist bottlers and retailers listed on pages 153-154. In particular, the Signatory bottlings include a stable of Silent Stills, drawn especially from this sad portfolio. Try and secure a bottle or two before it is too late.

DEFUNCT DISTILLERIES

BRAND	**Banff**
✉	BANFF, Banffshire
PRODUCTION STATUS	Closed 1983
ESTABLISHED	1863
🛢	Ex-bourbon

TASTING NOTES	1974, 40%
NOSE	Very light with a trace of smoke.
TASTE	Slightly aggressive, finishing a touch fiery. Nonetheless a good bite.
COMMENTS	A rare dram from a lost distillery. Seek out the vintages while you can. See pages 153-154.

BRAND	**Coleraine**
	✉ COLERAINE, Co. Antrim
PRODUCTION STATUS	Closed 1964. No longer exists.
ESTABLISHED	1820

AGE WHEN BOTTLED	34 years
STRENGTH ABV	57.1%

TASTING NOTES	Not available
COMMENTS	Literally extinct, the last bottles are now in collectors' hands. Expect to pay 'through the nose' if you can find one!

MALT	**Glen Albyn**
✉	INVERNESS, Inverness-shire
PRODUCTION STATUS	Closed 1983. Dismantled 1986.
ESTABLISHED	c1846
🛢	Ex-bourbon

TASTING NOTES	1972, 40%
NOSE	Light hint of sweetness and smoke with a fresh aroma.
TASTE	Well-rounded, malty and smoky with a full finish.
COMMENTS	See pages 153-154. Now a collector's item.

MALT	**Glen Mhor**
✉	INVERNESS, Inverness-shire
PRODUCTION STATUS	Closed 1983. Dismantled 1986.
ESTABLISHED	1892
🛢	Ex-bourbon

TASTING NOTES	12-year-old, 40%
NOSE	Light, sweet fragrance of hazelnuts.
TASTE	Light-bodied with a slight, toffee, dry finish.
COMMENTS	Another collector's dram. See pages 153-154.

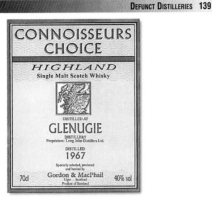

MALT	**Glenugie**
✉	PETERHEAD, Aberdeenshire
PRODUCTION STATUS	Closed 1983. No longer there.
ESTABLISHED	c1831
🛢	Ex-bourbon

TASTING NOTES	1967, 40%
NOSE	Hint of ripe fruit sweetness and a rich warmth.
TASTE	Initial trace of sweetness. Firm, smoky and malty but with a subtle, dry finish.
COMMENTS	A rare pre-dinner dram, see pages 153-154.

MALT	**Glenury-Royal**
✉	STONEHAVEN, Kincardineshire
OWNING COMPANY	UDV
PRODUCTION STATUS	Closed 1985. Will not reopen.
ESTABLISHED	c1825
SOURCE	Cowie Water
🛢	Ex-bourbon

TASTING NOTES	1978, 43%
NOSE	A light hint of smoke with a dry, fruity, fresh aroma.
TASTE	Light body with a dry, long, rich smoky finish.
COMMENTS	A good introductory malt, suitable for pre-dinner drinking but currently unavailable.

Established 1842

CADENHEAD'S

AUTHENTIC
COLLECTION

150th anniversary bottling

Single Malt Scotch Whisky

This whisky has been bottled from a selected individual cask
in its natural state and shows the character of that cask.
It has not been diluted with water. It has not been treated to
change its colour and is free from all additives. It has
not been subjected to any filtration that might remove
natural constituents and spoil its flavour.
It is the authentic product of its distillery.

Bottled by Wm. Cadenhead, 32 Union Street, Campbeltown,
SCOTLAND

From

KINCLAITH
Distillery

Distilled March 1965 and bottled December 1989
Matured in an oak cask

for **24** years

70cl   Product of Scotland   51.4%vol

MALT	**Kinclaith**
✉	Moffat Street, GLASGOW,
OWNING COMPANY	Last licensed to Long John Distillers
PRODUCTION STATUS	Dismantled 1975.
ESTABLISHED	1957-8

TASTING NOTES	18-year-old, 46%
NOSE	Light and smoky with a spirit sharpness.
TASTE	Full-bodied, smooth with an attractive finish.
COMMENTS	No longer with us and now in very limited supply. See pages 153-154.

MALT	**Millburn**
✉	INVERNESS, Inverness-shire
PRODUCTION STATUS	Closed 1985. Dismantled 1988.
ESTABLISHED	c1807
🛢	Ex-bourbon

TASTING NOTES	1972, 40%
NOSE	A rich aroma with a medium sweetness and a hint of smoke.
TASTE	Medium to full-bodied, a touch of fruit and a long finish which is both sweet and dry.
COMMENTS	Sadly, the last distillery to close in Inverness but the malt is still available. See pages 153-154.

CONNOISSEURS CHOICE

HIGHLAND
Single Malt Scotch Whisky

DISTILLED AT
NORTH PORT-BRECHIN
DISTILLERY
Proprietors: Mitchel Bros. Ltd
DISTILLED
1981

Specially selected, produced
and bottled by
Gordon & MacPhail
Elgin . Scotland
Product of Scotland

70cl   40% vol

MALT	**North Port**
✉	BRECHIN, Angus
OWNING COMPANY	UDV
PRODUCTION STATUS	Closed 1983. No longer there.
ESTABLISHED	c1820
SOURCE	Loch Lee
🛢	Ex-bourbon

TASTING NOTES	1974, 40%
NOSE	A light, sweet pronounced aroma with an astringent background.
TASTE	Starts sweet, but quickly fades to spirit – quite a pleasant, sharp tang.
COMMENTS	Pre-dinner, with a little water. See pages 153-154.

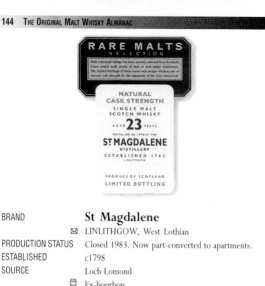

BRAND	**St Magdalene**
✉	LINLITHGOW, West Lothian
PRODUCTION STATUS	Closed 1983. Now part-converted to apartments.
ESTABLISHED	c1798
SOURCE	Loch Lomond
🛢	Ex-bourbon

AGE WHEN BOTTLED	23 years
STRENGTH ABV	58.1%

TASTING NOTES	1981, 40%
NOSE	Fresh, light, oaky sweetness. Smoky and dry – a real pot pourri of enhancing aromas.
TASTE	Sweet at first, developing to a smooth, well-balanced dryness with a smoky flavour which finishes slowly but ripely.
COMMENTS	A splash of water is essential. An excellent dram.

CLOSED DISTILLERIES

MALT	**Benromach**
✉	FORRES, Morayshire IV36 0EB
☎	01343-545111
🖷	01343-540155
OWNING COMPANY	Gordon & Macphail Ltd
PRODUCTION STATUS	Closed 1983. Being re-equipped by G&M.
ESTABLISHED	1898
SOURCE	Chapelton Springs
🥃	1
🝆	1

TASTING NOTES	1972, 40%
NOSE	Light, delicate and attractive with a fresh sweetness.
TASTE	Again, light and delicate but finishing with a pronounced maltiness and a long, dominant finish.
COMMENTS	A pre-dinner dram from a distillery which will soon commence distilling again. See pages 153-154.

RARE MALTS
SELECTION

Each individual vintage has been specially selected from Scotland's
finest single malt stocks of rare or now silent distilleries.
The limited bottlings of these unique and unusual whiskies are at
natural cask strength for the enjoyment of the true connoisseur.

NATURAL
CASK STRENGTH

SINGLE MALT
SCOTCH WHISKY

AGED **22** YEARS

DISTILLED IN 1972 AT THE

BRORA
DISTILLERY

ESTABLISHED 1819
BRORA SUTHERLAND

58.7%vol 70cl ℮

PRODUCE OF SCOTLAND
LIMITED BOTTLING

BRAND	**Brora**
✉	BRORA, Sutherland
OWNING COMPANY	UDV
PRODUCTION STATUS	Closed 1983. Will not reopen.
ESTABLISHED	1819
🛢	Ex-bourbon

AGE WHEN BOTTLED	22 years
STRENGTH ABV	60.0%

TASTING NOTES

NOSE
Full, enthralling flavour, peaty and rich with a subtle sweetness.

TASTE
Rich, smooth with an abundance of nutty, smoky flavours which linger on with a memorable sweetness.

COMMENTS
After-dinner dramming of outstanding quality. Remember that splash of water though! Probably the most fully flavoured whisky outside Islay at the moment. One of the UD Rare Malts Selection but almost unobtainable now.

MALT	**Coleburn**
✉	Longmorn, ELGIN, Morayshire
OWNING COMPANY	UDV
PRODUCTION STATUS	Closed 1985. Will not reopen.
ESTABLISHED	1897
SOURCE	Spring in the Glen of Rothes
🛢	Ex-bourbon
♨	2
♨	2

TASTING NOTES	1972, 40%
NOSE	Light and flowery with slight oily overtones which enhance the aroma.
TASTE	Light and pleasant with a well-rounded refreshing after-taste.
COMMENTS	Acquired by Distillers Company Ltd in 1930, it is representative of a typical small, two-still, late-Victorian distillery. See pages 153-154.

MALT	**Convalmore**
	✉ Dufftown, KEITH, Banffshire
OWNING COMPANY	Wm Grant & Sons Ltd
PRODUCTION STATUS	Closed 1985. Will not reopen.
ESTABLISHED	1894
SOURCE	Springs in the Conval Hills
	🛢 Ex-bourbon

TASTING NOTES	1969, 40%
NOSE	Light, aromatic heather aroma with a floral sweetness.
TASTE	Much more on the palate than the nose suggests. A pleasant, full, roundness which lingers longer than expected.
COMMENTS	An after-dinner malt. See pages 153-154.

MALT	**Glenesk**
✉	Hillside, MONTROSE, Angus
OWNING COMPANY	UDV
PRODUCTION STATUS	Closed 1985. Will not reopen.
ESTABLISHED	1897
SOURCE	River North Esk

AGE WHEN BOTTLED	12 years
STRENGTH ABV	40%
SPECIAL BOTTLINGS	1971, 25-y.o @ 62% Rare Malts Selection, bottled as Hillside.

TASTING NOTES	1984, 40%
NOSE	A light, delicate hint of sweetness.
TASTE	Quite full and sweet with a lingering finish, well balanced.
COMMENTS	After-dinner. The distillery was once known as North Esk and also as Hillside. Not an easy malt to find. See pages 153-154.

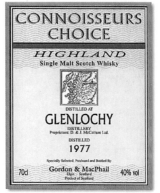

MALT	**Glenlochy**
✉	FORT WILLIAM, Inverness-shire
OWNING COMPANY	UDV
PRODUCTION STATUS	Closed 1983. Will not reopen.
ESTABLISHED	1898
SOURCE	River Nevis

TASTING NOTES	1974, 46%
NOSE	Light and aromatic with a hint of sweetness and fruit.
TASTE	Light, spicy flavour which tends to finish quickly.
COMMENTS	Pre-dinner drinking and becoming rarer. See pages 153-154.

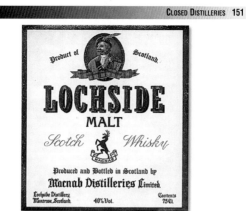

BRAND	**Lochside**
✉	Brechin Road, MONTROSE, Angus DD10 9AD
OWNING COMPANY	Last licensed to Allied Distillers Ltd
PRODUCTION STATUS	Closed 1991
ESTABLISHED	1957
SOURCE	Borehole aquifer
🛢	Ex-bourbon
🔥 2	
🔥 2	

AGE WHEN BOTTLED	10 years
STRENGTH ABV	40%

TASTING NOTES

NOSE — Light, aromatic with a delicate sweetness and a gentle background of dryness.

TASTE — Initially sweet, medium/dry with a lingering, stimulating effect and a long, gentle finish.

COMMENTS — Sadly this malt is now barely obtainable. The distillery's future is very bleak at present.

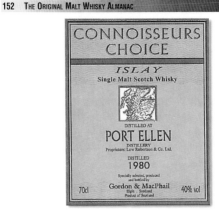

CONNOISSEURS CHOICE

ISLAY
Single Malt Scotch Whisky

DISTILLED AT
PORT ELLEN
DISTILLERY
Proprietors: Low Robertson & Co. Ltd.

DISTILLED
1980

Specially selected, produced
and bottled by
Gordon & MacPhail
Elgin - Scotland
Product of Scotland

70cl   40% vol

MALT	**Port Ellen**
✉	PORT ELLEN, Islay, Argyll PA42 7AJ
OWNING COMPANY	UDV
PRODUCTION STATUS	Closed 1983. Will not reopen.
ESTABLISHED	1825
SOURCE	Leorin Lochs
🛢	Ex-bourbon

TASTING NOTES	1980, 40%
NOSE	A touch peat with a delicate, sweet bouquet.
TASTE	Quite full and round with hints of smoke and a toffee-smooth finish.
COMMENTS	A fine, underrated dram. Direct exports to the Americas were first pioneered at Port Ellen in the 1840s. The associated industrial maltings now supply a great deal of Islay's malting requirement. See pages 153-154.

Independent Bottlers
and Specialist Retailers

I have included two more independent bottlers in this section along with 13 specialist retailers who offer a reliable service in supplying fine malts. Due to the ever-changing nature of their lists, I am no longer detailing specific vintages. If you are looking for a particular malt, simply phone any of the contacts below for more information.

With regard to the high street, Oddbins continue to source superb malts from a range of producers and their staff are always enthusiastic and willing to chat about the subject as well.

Independent Bottlers

GORDON & MACPHAIL LTD
George House
Boroughbriggs Road
ELGIN, Morayshire IV30 1JY
☎ 01343-545111
📠 01343-540155
Contact: Marketing department

CADENHEADS WHISKY SHOP
172 Canongate
EDINBURGH EH8 8BN
☎ 0131-556-5864
📠 0131-556-2527
(retail and mixed cases)
☎ 01586-554258 (wholesale)
Contact: Craig Clapperton

THE VINTAGE MALT WHISKY CO LTD
2 Stewart Street
MILNGAVIE G62 6BW
☎ 0141-955-1700
📠 0141-955-1701
http://www.vintage-malt-whisky.co.uk
Contact: Brian Crook

MURRAY MCDAVID
56 Walton Street
LONDON SW3 1RB
☎ 0171-823-7717
📠 0171-581-0250
Contact: Gordon Wright

SIGNATORY VINTAGE SCOTCH WHISKY CO LTD
7/8 Elizafield
Newhaven Road, EDINBURGH EH6 5PY
☎ 0131-555-4988
📠 0131-555-5211
Contact: Andrew or Brian Symington

Specialist Retailers

LONDON

CADENHEADS WHISKY SHOP
3 Russell Street
Covent Garden, LONDON WC2B 5JD
☎ 0171-379-46404
📠 0171-379-4600
(retail and mixed cases)
☎ 01586-554258 (wholesale)
Contact: Sean Ivers

MILROYS OF SOHO
3 Greek Street
Soho, LONDON W1V 6NX
☎ 0171-437-0893
📠 0171-437-1345
Contact: Doug McIvor, Bridget Arthur

FORTNUM & MASON
181 Piccadilly
LONDON W1A ER
☎ 0171-734-8040
📠 0171-437-3278
Contact: Annette Duce

HARRODS LTD
Knightsbridge
LONDON SW1X 7XL
☎ 0171-730-1234 ext 3162
📠 0171-225-5823
Contact: Alistair Viner

SELFRIDGES LTD
400 Oxford Street
LONDON W1A 1AB
☎ 0171-318-3730
📠 0171-491-1880
Contact: Colin Akers

THE NEST
106/108 Uxbridge Road
Hanwell, LONDON W7 3SU
☎ 0181-579-7273
📠 0181-840-9431
Contact: Sukindar Singh

THE VINTAGE HOUSE
42 Old Compton Street
Soho, LONDON W1V 6LR
☎ 0171-437-2592
📠 0171-734-1174
http://www.vintagehouse.co.uk
Contact: Michael Mullin or Michael Barton.

ENGLAND

THE WRIGHT WINE COMPANY
The Old Smithy, Raikes Road
SKIPTON, North Yorkshire BD23 1NP
☎ 01756-700886
📠 01756-798580
Contact: Julian Kaye

TANNER'S WINES
26 Wyle Cop
SHREWSBURY, Shropshire SY1 1XD
☎ 01743-234455
📠 01743-234501
Contact: John Melhuish

SCOTLAND

CAIRNGORM WHISKY CENTRE
Inverdruie, AVIEMORE, Inverness-shire
PH22 1QH
☎ & 📠 01479-810574
Contact: Frank Clark

LOCH FYNE WHISKIES
INVERARAY, Argyll PA32 8UD
☎ 01499-302219
📠 01499-302238
http: //www.lfw.co.uk
Contact: Richard Joynson

LUVIAN'S BOTTLE SHOP
93 Bonnygate
CUPAR, Fife KY15 4LG
☎ & 📠 01334-654820
Contact: Vince Fusaro

MOFFAT WINE SHOP
8 Well Street
MOFFAT, Dumfriesshire DG10 9DP
☎ 01683- 220554
Contact: Tony McIlwrick

GERMANY

SCOTCH MALT WHISKY GmbH
26441 Jever
AM BULLHAMM 17
☎ 044-61-912237
📠 044-61-912239
E-mail: scoma@T-Online.de

Whisky on the Web

H ere are some of the more interesting Websites on the subject of Scotch whisky currently available on the Internet. I accept no responsibility for their contents but I hope you find them very informative.

Generic sites

http://www.islaywhisky.com

http://www.scotchwhisky.com

http://www.scotch-whisky.org.uk
(Scotch Whisky Association)

http://www.whiskeypages.com
(*Malt Advocate* Magazine)

http://www.whiskyweb.com

http://www.whisky.de

Retailers

http://www.whiskyshop.com
(The Whisky Shop, Scotland)

http://www.lfw.co.uk

http://www.thewhiskyhouse.com

http://www.vintagehouse.co.uk

http://www.whisky.de/scoma.htm

http://www.smws.com
(Scotch Malt Whisky Society)

Brands – Malt

http://www.themacallan-themalt.com

http://www.glenmorangie.com

http://www.glengoyne.com

http://www.glenord.com

http://www.laphroaig.com

http://www.glenfiddich.com

Brands – Blends

http://www.cutty-sark.com

http://www.famousgrouse.com

http://www.chivas.com

http://www.hankeybannister.com

http://www.cattos.com

http://www.dewars.co.uk

http://www.blackbottle.com

http://www.buchanans.com

http://www.ballantines.com

Whisky Liqueurs

http://www.wallace-malt.co.uk

http://www.drambuie.com

Corporate and Company

http://www.scotch.com
(United Distillers & Vintners)

http://www.inverhouse.com

http://www.ianmacleod.com

http://www.jb.aed.es/
(J&B Jet)

http://www.ballantines-es.com/

http://cutty.varma.es/
(Cutty Sark)

http://www.ballantines.de/

The Keepers of the Quaich

The Keepers of the Quaich is an exclusive, internationally recognised Society with members in over 60 countries worldwide. Membership, by invitation only, is granted to those with a positive record of contribution to the international success of Scotch whisky.

When the Society was established by the major companies in the industry to build on the image and worldwide prestige of Scotch whisky, they pooled their enormous resources and strengths to promote Scotch with pride.

As a Scotch whisky institution, charitable donations are, from time to time, made to worthwhile causes benefitting Scotland and its people.

All Keepers have one fundamental link in common – a love of Scotland and Scotch whisky.

Mission statement

'To advance the standing and prosperity of one of Britain's premier export industries, and to make more widely known its uniqueness, traditions, quality, service and benefits to the community it serves at home and in the markets of the world.'

Patrons

The Rt. Hon. The Earl of Erroll, His Grace The Duke of Argyll J.P., His Grace The Duke of Atholl, The Rt. Hon. The Earl of Elgin & Kincardine K.T., The Rt. Hon. The Earl of Mansfield D.L., J.P., Sir Iain Tennant K.T., LLD, The Rt. Hon. The Lord Macfarlane of Bearsden K.T., Mrs James Troughton, Sir George Bull and The Viscount Thurso.

Founding partners

Allied Distillers Ltd
2 Glasgow Road
DUMBARTON G82 1ND

Incorporating George Ballantine & Son, William Teacher & Sons, Stewart & Son of Dundee and Long John International, this company formed in January 1988 controls the Scotch whisky interests of Allied Domecq PLC. Headquartered in Dumbarton, the company, which operates two large grain distilleries and 12 malt distilleries, continues an association with the town first started in 1938 by Hiram Walker.

United Distillers & Vintners
33 Ellersly Road
EDINBURGH EH12 6JW
and
8 Henrietta Place
LONDON W1M 9AG

United Distillers & Vintners, which is the spirits division of Diageo plc, was formed following the merger of Grand Metropolitan and Guinness and the combination of International Distillers and Vintners and United Distillers. The company is the world's leading producer of branded spirits in the UK and 19 of its brands rank in the top 100 international spirits including Johnnie Walker, Bell's Extra Special and White Horse Scotch whiskies.

Justerini & Brooks Ltd
8 Henrietta Place
LONDON W1M 9AG

This company was founded in 1749 by Giacomo Justerini, an Italian cordial maker who came to London in pursuit of an opera singer. He failed in his quest for the lady, but remained to form a commercial alliance with George Johnson and together they set themselves up as wine merchants. By 1760 the company had been granted the first of its eight successive Royal Warrants and in 1830 the company was bought by Alfred Brooks. A century later the house brand of Scotch whisky – J&B Rare dominated the company's exports to the United States. After merging with Twiss Browning and Hallowes to form United Wine Traders, the company bought Gilbey's in 1962 to form International Distillers and Vintners, the drinks division of Grand Metropolitan plc. In 1998 Grand Metropolitan merged with Guinness PLC to form Diageo and the spirit division was combined with that of United Distillers to form United Distillers and Vintners.

Highland Distillers Co plc
West Kinfauns
PERTH PH2 7XZ
and
The Edrington Group Ltd
106 West Nile Street
GLASGOW G1 2QY

The Highland Distilleries Company was incorporated in July 1887 as distillers of high quality malt whisky for the blending trade having secured the ownership of both Glenrothes and Bunnahabhain distilleries. Having acquired Glenglassaugh distillery in 1892 and Tamdhu in 1898, the company expanded its interests and later formed a close association with whisky brokers Robertson & Baxter Ltd. The portfolio was enlarged with the addition of Highland

Park in Orkney in 1937 and its blended whisky interests were also furthered with the take-over of Matthew Gloag & Son Ltd, the Perth blenders of The Famous Grouse in 1970. Black Bottle was added to the company's portfolio in 1995 and The Macallan in 1996 when Highland Distilleries acquired the majority shareholding in Macallan-Glenlivet PLC.

Chivas Brothers Ltd
The Ark
201 Talgarth Road
LONDON W6 8BN

Chivas Brothers Ltd was founded in Aberdeen in 1801 as a fine grocery business. James Chivas joined in 1836 and within five years had taken over the enterprise as his own. The specialist Scotch whisky blending aspect of the business developed during the 1840s and 1850s and by the 1890s Chivas Brothers had created what was to become the world's leading premium Scotch whisky brand – Chivas Regal. This was first exported to the United States in 1909, and is still at the very forefront of the Chivas Brothers' brand portfolio. In 1949 Chivas Brothers was acquired by Seagram Distillers Plc.

Chivas Brothers today is responsible for the global strategic marketing direction and business development of Chivas Brothers' Scotch whisky brands. The Chivas Brothers' brands, led by Chivas Regal 12-year-old and Royal Salute 21-year-old, also include Chivas Regal 18-year-old, Chivas Brothers' the Century of Malts, Chivas Brothers 1801 and Strathisla Pure Highland Malt.

In addition, Chivas Brothers is also responsible for the production and asset management of the entire Seagram Scotch whisky portfolio including The Glenlivet, Glen Grant, Passport and Something Special.

CORPORATE MEMBERS

Berry Bros & Rudd Ltd
3 St James's Street
LONDON SW1A 1EG

Burn Stewart Distillers PLC
8 Milton Road
College Milton North
EAST KILBRIDE G74 5BU

Campbell Distillers Ltd
West Byrehill
KILWINNING KA13 6LE

The Drambuie Liqueur Company Ltd
Stirling Road
KIRKLISTON
West Lothian EH29 9EE

J&G Grant
Glenfarclas Distillery
Marypark
BALLINDALLOCH
Banffshire AB3 9BD

William Grant & Sons Ltd
Independence House
84 Lower Mortlake Road
RICHMOND
Surrey TW9 2HS

Inver House Distillers Ltd
Towers Road
AIRDRIE ML6 8PL

William Lawson Distillers Ltd
288 Main Street
COATBRIDGE ML5 3RH

The Macallan Distillers Ltd
CRAIGELLACHIE
Banffshire AB3 9RX

Glenmorangie plc
Macdonald House
18 Westerton Road
BROXBURN
West Lothian EH52 5AQ

Morrison Bowmore Distillers Ltd
Springburn Bond
Carlisle Street
GLASGOW G21 1EQ

The Tomatin Distillery Co Ltd
TOMATIN IV13 7YT

JBB (Greater Europe) PLC
Dalmore House
310 St Vincent Street
GLASGOW G2 5RG

Index of Malts